*The Reality
   of the Gospel
and the Unreality
   of the Churches*

The Reality
of the Gospel
and the Unreality
of the Churches

by DOUGLAS JOHN HALL

THE WESTMINSTER PRESS

PHILADELPHIA

Scripture quotations from the Revised Standard
Version of the Bible are copyright, 1946 and
1952, by the Division of Christian Education
of the National Council of Churches,
and are used by permission.

BOOK DESIGN BY DOROTHY E. JONES

PUBLISHED BY THE WESTMINSTER PRESS ®
PHILADELPHIA, PENNSYLVANIA

PRINTED IN THE UNITED STATES OF AMERICA

Library of Congress Cataloging in Publication Data

Hall, Douglas John, 1928–
    The reality of the Gospel and the unreality of the
churches.

    Includes bibliographical references.
    1. Church and the world. 2. Christianity—20th
century. I. Title.
BR115.W6H34   261.8   75–12852
ISBN 0–664–24775–X

To my Students, Colleagues, and Associates
at St. Andrew's College, 1965–1975

Contents

Preface

These chapters grew out of lectures for parish ministers in a course at McGill University, Montreal.

At the end of the lectures, one of the ministers thanked me on behalf of the others. I was a little surprised to hear him say, "You are a theologian who cares about the churches."

It was not the sort of thing I had become accustomed to hearing. Quite the opposite, in fact. Like most teachers of theology, I have been rather critical of the churches. And usually this criticism has produced a predictably defensive response from church-committed laymen and clergy. It was therefore wonderfully surprising to hear this spokesman for clergy of several denominations tell me, "You care about the churches." It is true. I do care about them.

It seems to me unfortunate that professional theolo-

gians on the whole have assumed an attitude of indifference toward the churches. "Leave them to heaven!"
seems to be the general approach. And in the meantime
let us get on with the important and interesting task of
theology.

So the fate of the churches is left, not really to heaven,
but to persons who have little disciplined theological
reflection. Many of these people are excited enough, to
be sure. They are turned on by the concept of "Change"
and the dynamics of this concept. Grand schemes are
worked out in head offices. Overnight, whole ecclesiastical departments disappear—only to be replaced by
similar entities under different names.

Sometimes, the devotees of "Change" have grasped
something of the vastness of the upheaval through
which Western civilization is passing. But this awareness is hardly ever allowed to mature. If it were, the
whole bureaucratic ecclesiastical structure, which perpetuates itself by continuous rearrangement (*not* Reformation!), would be called into question.

There is a commitment to the fundamental patterns
of churchly existence, firmly established over the centuries, which guarantees that most official ecclesiastical
contemplation of the Christian situation today will
limit itself to superficial observation. The change that
is contemplated is the sort of "Change" that is deemed
necessary for the institutional churches to survive. But,
in the last analysis, that "Change" will be little more
than "rearranging the deck chairs on the *Titanic,*" as a
colleague of mine has aptly phrased it.

As a theologian I am concerned about the churches
because I am concerned about the church. I do not find
it possible—some of my professional colleagues appar-

ently do—to make a clear-cut separation between the churches and the church. If the churches fail—that is, if they prove incapable of reforming themselves in response to the contemporary needs of mankind and to the call of the Spirit—then that failure is bound to shape the life of the future church. It is absurd to meditate with theological rapture on the coming great church and in the meantime to leave the churches to heaven and the Change-makers. If there is a church in the future—or if what there is is somehow more nearly the church than what we have now—it will be in large measure because of decisions and deeds undertaken right now in and by the churches.

Since my object in this little study has been to speak to and to serve the churches, I have not attempted to make it a polished and learned theological treatise. I do not think that it is condescending, theologically or intellectually. It will require careful attention on the part of the reader; at some points it is even more academic than I could wish. But it is intended for ordinary Christians, ministers and laymen, without specialized theological experience—the persons who must decide, in the long run, what will become of the churches. I have the impression that more of them are anxious to have some help from the theologians today than ever before.

D.J.H.

McGill University
Montreal, Canada

Introduction

Two experiences are almost universal among Christians throughout the Western world today. These two experiences conflict with each other, and they are usually felt most acutely by the most thoughtful people. So it is not surprising that an atmosphere of frustration prevails in places where Christian faith is taken seriously.

On the one hand, sensitive Christians experience a new openness to the basic elements of faith on the part of many secular persons. Apparently it is possible again for some of our worldly neighbors to think now and then that the Christian gospel might have something to do with the real world. This in turn gives many of us Christians the courage to enter the real world, believing that what we have to bear witness to may actually be pertinent to its condition, after all!

On the other hand, there is the conflicting experience of a vacuum, an emptiness, an absence of reality in the churches. Sometimes it seems more sinister than a mere absence. Those who become most conscious of it often suspect that it is a deliberate pursuit of unreality.

This sense of the unreality of the churches is most frequently expressed, not by outsiders, but by persons closely associated with the churches. Often by ministers, priests, and conscientious laypersons. In a recent study of clergy who left the parish ministry, an editor of the report writes, "There is a strong feeling [among these ex-pastors] concerning a lack of reality in the church, and the implication that those who are outside the church are more real than those who are inside."[1] This feeling is by no means confined to those who *leave* the ministry, nor to clergy.

What makes it all so frustrating is the simple, incontrovertible fact that the unreality of the churches *militates against* the possibility that the new openness to the reality of the gospel will find a sympathetic and informed Christian presence with which to enter into dialogue. While the world sharpens its questions—and is pierced to the heart by them!—the churches seem to keep people insulated from all desperate questions. They provide the impression that there are, after all, no unanswerable questions.

Sometimes I reflect on this situation in the metaphor of the Biblical story about Nicodemus, who came to Jesus by night:

Every Christian who has gone far enough into the night of the human condition has encountered a fair share of Nicodemuses. They come to him quietly, without much fanfare, asking whether they can expect any light in this "encircling gloom." Often they emerge out of surprising places. Who would have expected *such* people to appear? They seemed secure enough a decade or so ago. Secular people, a little bored in a world without mystery. Scientists, who only yesterday would not have demeaned themselves by speaking with philosophers, let alone theologians! Dialectical materialists, who ask for a little spirit, a little . . . transcendence! Humanists who have run short of faith in man. Ordinary men and women, who think a little and are afraid of what they think. It is not unusual to encounter these Nicodemuses in today's night.

The condition for such encounters, however, is that one has to have gone far enough into the night himself. The Nicodemuses do not appear to Christians who live only in the light! And so I wonder: For how many Nicodemuses is there no one, in the night, to—I will not say to answer, but at least to listen?

The purpose of this study, accordingly, is to reflect on these two conflicting experiences. What lies behind the new appreciation for the worldly realism of the gospel on the part of many who formerly would have turned away? And why, at the very moment when the gospel begins to seem almost real again, does so much about the churches seem unreal?

But I am not interested only in reflection and analysis. I also want to be able to act and to help others to act. Therefore I am trying to understand whether, and how, the churches could be delivered from this reputation for unreality. Could the churches be swept up into the reality of the gospel? What would it mean for the churches to be subjected to the scrutiny and purification of a gospel that is ready for new dialogue with the contemporary world? What would have to go and what would have to be gained, for the churches to be "there" for the encounter with Nicodemus in his extremity?

Because that is the primary object of these observations, I intend that everything should press toward the final chapter. No such discussion as this could possibly encompass, or even envisage, all the concrete things that are entailed by the basic proposal of that chapter. Nevertheless I hope that it will be received as an exercise in *practical* theology.

To many, no doubt, it will seem fuzzy, visionary, and quite *im*practical. But practicability is frequently nothing more than the preoccupation of those who resist change, particularly fundamental change. For all who fear visions I should like to cite a representative of that branch of human wisdom which most enshrines our culture's concern for the pragmatic and the practical. In the final paragraph of his learned study of the physical crises of our biosphere, the scientist Paul Ehrlich provides the following "conclusion":

> Perhaps the major necessary ingredient that has been missing from a solution to the problems of both the United States and the rest of the world is a goal, a vision of the kind of Spaceship Earth that ought to be and the kind of crew that should man her. Society has always had its visionaries who talked of love, beauty, peace and plenty. But somehow the "practical" men have always been there to praise the smog as a sign of progress, to preach "just" wars, and to restrict love while giving hate free rein. It must be one of the greatest ironies of the history of *Homo sapiens* that the only salvation for the practical men now lies in what they think of as the dreams of idealists. The question now is: can the "realists" be persuaded to face reality in time?[2]

Ehrlich wants to introduce authentic realism into our thinking about the world at large. My object here is more modest: I only want the churches to become real, that is, to become the church.

Chapter 1

The Reality
of the Gospel

INTRODUCTION

"Can the World Be Saved?"

Five or six years ago I was preparing a seminar on "Theology of the Future." I found myself one afternoon flipping through the pages of a magazine I had never looked at before. Suddenly my attention was caught by the bold letters of an article entitled "Can the World Be Saved?"

Such a title would not have surprised me at all if the publication in my hands had been *The Watchtower* of the Jehovah's Witnesses. But it wasn't anything like that. It was the learned journal *Bio-Science*.

That a respected medium of scientific research and opinion should be found raising the question of salvation could not have been predicted at the turn of this century. Few intellectuals would have thought it sane to put such a question prior to World War I. And in North America one would be hard pressed to find refer-

ence to anything vaguely reminiscent of that question
—in that context—up to and including World War II.

Let's face it: even among the religious such a bald
statement of the soteriological question (Can the World
Be *Saved?*) has been regarded as somehow distasteful
and lacking in sophistication. It is the sort of thing that
might be expected from the lunatic fringe of the
church. Even the religious have learned how to interpret salvation in immanental, historical, or downright
secular terms. It is a process, a movement within history, or history itself, in its progressive march toward
the Kingdom of God!

William Temple, the great English churchman, made
a statement in 1938 which reflects that interpretation of
salvation. Yet, because he was sensitive to the times in
which he was living, he was able to see beyond his times
into ours. He wrote, almost wistfully:

> If we began our work again today, its perspectives would
> be different. . . .
>
> I am conscious of a certain transition of interest in
> our minds, as in the minds of theologians all over the
> world. . . .
>
> If the security of the nineteenth century, already shat-
> tered in Europe, finally crumbles away in our country, we
> shall be pressed more and more towards a theology of
> Redemption. . . .
>
> A theology of Redemption . . . tends . . . to sound the
> prophetic note; it is more ready to admit that much in this
> evil world is irrational and strictly unintelligible. . . .
>
> [If such becomes our emphasis] we shall be coming
> closer to the New Testament. We have been learning again
> how impotent man is to save himself, how deep and perva-
> sive is that corruption which theologians call Original Sin.

Man needs above all else to be saved from himself. This must be the work of Divine Grace.[3]

Archbishop Temple predicts a time in which *Christians* (even English Christians!) will again ask about a possible redemption of the world from beyond its own resources. I wonder whether he might not have been astonished to discover that in only three or four decades *the world itself* would be asking after that possibility? Not only the pious but also the profane, and even the most exalted representatives of the profane, are asking whether the world can still be "saved." And they are asking it with a certain desperation.

➺ 1 ᔕ

A NEW OPENNESS TO THE GOSPEL

The Death of Man

The demise of man's confidence in himself and in history has occasioned a new openness to a religion of redemption. "Man is in his death throes," wrote Gabriel Marcel.[4] In his desperation, he looks about wildly for healing, or even for an understanding of the disease that is killing him. For he does not even comprehend this disease.

How could he? Nothing in his indoctrination, nothing in the past that he can rightly remember, nothing in the future for which he was taught to hope, can give him a clue to this suffering. At his most insightful he feels it as a loss of nerve or of hope. It is a matter of thwarted expectations. His expectations were great ones, and now they are everywhere contradicted by his experience.

Modernity conditioned him to expect the triumph of reason, and he inherited instead the triumph of technique. Technique reduces rationality to a process that moves inexorably toward the mastery of all unpredictable and inefficient elements, a process that therefore cannot permit freedom and dignity in its initiator.[5] Modernity promised him peace everlasting, with himself as peacemaker, and he reaped Vietnam. Modernity taught him to expect the moon, and he got the moon. But it was cold and empty, and his words were empty words, as he planted his feet and his flag upon it.[6] Modernity spoke only about progress. The word "regress" was dropped from the nineteenth-century vocabulary, and without that word it is hard to express much of what we feel about contemporary life. "Closed in the name of *Progress!*" declared the handwriting on the blackboard in the little red schoolhouse that my brother bought recently, the schoolhouse to which my mother went daily as a child, and later on I myself. The word "Progress" had been heavily underlined, with evident ironic intent.

The irony of progress is a typical theme, not only of our unguarded public and private talk, but of our art. In Karel Čapek's play *R.U.R.*, we hear the following dialogue between Alquist, the only remaining human being to survive the final rebellion of the robots, and Helena, the heroine of the story:

HELENA: . . . Don't you ever feel nervous?
ALQUIST: Well, ma'am, I'm an old man, you know. I'm not very fond of progress and these newfangled ideas.

HELENA: Like Emma? [the robot maid, who is religious]

ALQUIST: Yes, like Emma. Has Emma got a prayer book?

HELENA: Yes, a big, thick one.

ALQUIST: And has it got prayers for various occasions? Against thunderstorms? Against illness?

HELENA: Against temptations, against floods—

ALQUIST: And not against progress?

HELENA: I don't think so.

ALQUIST: That's a pity.

HELENA: Would you like to pray?

ALQUIST: I do pray.

HELENA: How?

ALQUIST: Something like this: "O Lord, I thank Thee for having wearied me. God, enlighten Domain [manager of the robot works] and all those who are astray; destroy their work, and aid mankind to return to their labors; preserve them from destruction; let them not suffer harm to soul or body; deliver us from the Robots, and protect Helena. Amen."[7]

Post-industrial, post-revolutionary, post-progressive man learns again, sometimes, to pray. His prayer is not pious, and it is not confident. In fact, it is not prayer in the usual understanding. It seldom gets as far as God, since it is so preoccupied with the plight of man. But there is in it a deep sighing and groaning, like the groaning of the "whole creation" about which the apostle Paul spoke (Rom. 8:22). Elemental prayer. An almost biological groaning, in which, if there is no explicitly religious "feeling after" the divine (Acts, ch. 17), there is at least the implicit recognition of our human need. The recognition that "we are beggars."[8] That recognition, as Schleiermacher knew, is the necessary precondition for openness to a religion of redemption. It always has been.

The Articulate Minority

This is not to suggest that the awareness of our "absolute dependence" (Schleiermacher) is present today in every man, or even in the majority. Certainly it is not present in the majority at the conscious level. One suspects that the disease of contemporary man is so frightening to him—and all the more so because he cannot comprehend it—that most men do what is usually done in such cases: They blot out the awareness of it. They repress it from their consciousness. And they suppress all those whose words or deeds, or whose very presence, brings the disease to mind. Again and again, and from every quarter, we are accused of being a "repressive society." What is meant by the wisest of those who make this diagnosis is that we are a society which cannot openly confront its own beggarliness. The disease is not that we are beggars, but that we cannot *admit* that we are beggars. To sustain our vision of ourselves as independent and good, we are not above disowning our own offspring, not even above approving policemen who beat and kill them. Besides, there are powerful institutions that are glad to assist in the implementing of this repressive process.

Although the response of the majority to the apocalyptic groaning of the age is one of repression, a great many of our contemporaries have been able to rise above repression. If there is a Silent Majority, there is also an Articulate Minority.

Often they are the most sensitive, the most committed to earth and man. The artists—all the arts[9]—have been courageously exploring the malaise of modern civilization for decades now, even for a century and more. Now these poets, the latter-day Jobs, are joined by Jeremiahs who possess impressive credentials: scientists, economists, sociologists, and even (perhaps especially!) a reflective minority of technologists, who are able from within to glimpse aspects of the technocratic humiliation of man.

Scientists, who have happened upon the world "problematique" rather recently without much preparation, often exhibit in their own behavior the pathos of contemporary man. I will not soon forget the young scientist who was a colleague of mine in an interdisciplinary course in our university. Incidentally, this was the *only* interdisciplinary course in this large university; for the way of repression also fears what may happen when men *pool* their awareness of the world. He stood in front of the class after his lecture, answering questions. The questions became accusations. Why had all this happened? What was the meaning of this pollution—yes, this deliberate destruction of "our" world? Is this what the generation in authority wants to bequeath to us? Is this the legacy of science?

The scientist kept backing away from this onslaught. At last he couldn't retreat any farther. He was cornered. "Look!" he exclaimed, like some trapped animal. "I'm only somebody who was interested in bugs. An entomologist, as one says. I was curious, you see, about the world of the bugs. It was fine at first. Then a few years ago I began to be aware of it: there was something wrong in the world of the bugs. Drastically wrong. What could it be? I tried to track it down, this deadly enemy of the bugs. At last I found out who it was. It was I myself. I and my species—*Homo sapiens!*—we are the enemy of the bugs. . . . And I haven't a clue what to do about *that* problem. Nobody ever told me how to un-

derstand *me*—not as a problem, anyway." He seemed to
me visibly broken.

Not only the scientists, however, but most of those
persons in whom consciousness of the human predicament is most acute today suffer deeply for their knowledge. Their suffering stems partly from the fact that
their testimony is regularly dismissed by the dominant
culture. Their refusal to play the game of repression
makes them objects of scorn and rejection in such a
society. This rejection can take many subtle forms, all
the way from personal alienation to the failure to
achieve tenure or promotions. Their suffering is also
and more profoundly the consequence of their determination to pursue truth, no matter how devastating it
may be.

Hermann Hesse speaks of this latter suffering in his
novel *Steppenwolf,* which not accidentally became almost a bible of the counter culture five or six years ago.
In the agonized journals of Herr Haller, the protago-
nist, the novelist wants us to see

> not the eccentricity of a single individual, but the sickness
> of the times themselves, the neurosis of that generation to
> which Haller belongs, a sickness, it seems, that by no
> means attacks the weak and worthless only but, rather,
> precisely those who are strongest in spirit and richest in
> gifts.[10]

Unfortunately the impression has been created that
those who writhe under the yoke of such knowledge
represent a mere handful of persons. In part, this impression is due to some elements within the Articulate
Minority itself, who thrive on the sense of their own
uniqueness. Perhaps they fancy themselves an elite.

Perhaps they enjoy persecution. But whatever the explanation, it is a wrong impression. It may have been the case at the end of the nineteenth century that those who protested against the dominant culture were a mere handful. Nietzsche thought that he was all alone in his condemnation of his epoch. Kierkegaard *was*, practically. But what Kierkegaard, Nietzsche, Freud, Dickens, Marx, and even Shakespeare, saw in advance of their time a very significant minority has grasped at varying levels in our time. This minority can no longer be dismissed by naming it "the Beats," or "the Hippies," or "the Communists."

Nicodemus is a movement.

Marcuse called the movement "the Great Refusal," and some identified it with the counter culture. There have been and will be other attempts to label it. Perhaps it is better not to call it anything at all. Obviously it is diverse, amorphous, disconnected. It is a revolutionary energy that transcends all the little revolutions of our epoch, while at the same time giving them whatever power they have. It is not at all clear that this energy can finally form itself into something sufficiently unified to represent an alternative. There are constant rumors that it has already dissipated, or been absorbed. That seems to me a shortsighted judgment. It takes too little account of the long history of this revolution of the depths. It too easily equates the protest movement with one of its manifestations—notably the counter culture of the '60s, in which a dimension of this movement assumed a particularly colorful and conspicuous form.

Whatever else may be said about it, this Articulate Minority is one in its judgment that our way of life is a way of death. It seeks another way, a way into the future, beyond the impasse of modernity. It asks whether the world can be "saved."

Wherever this question is put, explicitly or implicitly, there is a new openness to a religion of redemption. In the context of this question the Christian gospel is always potentially real, even for those who self-consciously reject Christianity. The question is: Are there Christians who can rise to this occasion?

The Scandal Remains

Let me introduce an important nuance.

When I refer to the new reality of the gospel, I do *not* mean that the gospel of Jesus Christ has suddenly become immediately and easily applicable to life.

There are people in our midst who have jumped to that conclusion. There are always rather macabre religious persons, ecclesiastical vultures, who feed on the death of man. They will quote with approval the adage, "Man's extremity is God's opportunity," and thus take a certain delight in the fall of man's "tragic empires." Unlike God who, according to the Scriptures, is by no means elated over the downfall of Babylon (Rev., chs. 14 to 18).

Something of this macabre attitude seems to me to inform the so-called charismatic movement. No doubt it can be quite exhilarating to witness all those virile young people, potential revolutionaries, laying down their lives in abject humiliation, turning off their minds in order to turn on their spirits, rejecting the world of deed and word for the spirit world of tongues and sexless togetherness! For those who shepherd such a flock there can be a good deal of generational revenge in it.

What has to be questioned more seriously, however,

is the way in which this movement sets aside the scandal of the gospel by capitalizing on the secular apocalypse. In an atmosphere of cataclysmic finality, so keenly felt by many of the young especially, it becomes possible to overlook the difficulties of belief that have been the common experience of thinking people for at least two or three centuries. The offense of the gospel is brushed aside, and everything from the virgin birth to the physical resurrection of the Christ becomes immediately acceptable and meaningful.

Such movements should not be lightly dismissed. Behind them lies the pathos and anguish of men and women, many of them young, for whom historical existence has become extremely painful. It is precisely this quite human desire to escape from the pain of history that gives fundamentalist and otherworldly religion its new opportunity for converts today. Anyone deeply involved in the problematic of the age can sympathize with the temptation to flee history. But the Christian gospel only provides such a possibility when it is badly distorted.

For whatever else the Christian message may mean, it means centrally that redemption is offered to *this* world. It is not an offer of salvation *out of* the world. It hopes to rescue men from bondage *to* the world, but in order that they may become more "fully alive" (Irenaeus) *in* the world. Like all religion, Christianity easily becomes the vehicle of man's propensity to escape his humanity, to create a secondary world that permits him to abandon this one without anxiety or guilt. But faith that takes God's own assumption of our humanity as its central claim can only lend itself to the human need to escape by denying its own chief affirmation: the incarnation. It is precisely this ("good") world that the God of Abraham, Isaac, and Jacob, the Father of Jesus Christ, wants to save.

When I speak of a new openness to the gospel, then, I am not drawing primarily on the experience of those who have found in Jesus Christ or in the Spirit the same sort of flight from existence that others have found in drugs, sex, or highly Westernized Eastern religions. It is true that the same condition which has made it possible for "the old-time religion" to win new converts today provides the opportunity for persons like me, who reject this "old-time religion," to point to a new openness to the gospel. But the way in which I permit myself to reflect upon that openness, and to meet those in whom it is manifest, is quite different from what occurs among the advocates of this or that version of "the old-time religion."

Primarily the difference is this: I take it as given that the *skandalon* of the gospel will be experienced just as much today as ever before. It is given, I believe, in both the theological and the historical-sociological senses.

The essence of the "scandal" is still what it was for Paul—the cross. Christian faith dares to assert that the redemption it proclaims is precisely redemption *of this world*. This redemption is being, has been, and shall be brought about through the suffering of one man, Jesus. If Christian faith confined itself to heaven, to the salvation of souls, to preparation for the next world (which is admittedly what the Christian religion has mostly busied itself with), then it would not be at all scandalous, really. The world knows perfectly well how to live happily with religions that offer such an opiate. But the world is offended, deeply hurt, by a faith that claims the possibility of wholeness for earth, for the flesh, for history, for bodies! Man is "scandalized" by such an offer, not because he does not desire it, but because he desires it so greatly. Yet he does not trust it. How could he believe himself worth so much?

Contemporary man is even more susceptible to the *skandalon* of the gospel than were our forefathers, or those to whom Paul first wrote in these terms (I Cor. 1:23). Why wouldn't he be? He has been instructed to regard himself as a "naked ape," a "sexual twitch," and other things far surpassing in worthlessness Calvin's definition of man as "a worm five feet high." In pre-Nazi Germany, reports Abraham Heschel, the following definition of man was frequently quoted:

> The human body contains a sufficient amount of fat to make seven cakes of soap, enough iron to make a medium sized nail, a sufficient amount of phosphorus to equip two thousand match heads, enough sulphur to rid oneself of fleas.[11]

The redemption of our bodies? What a bitter joke! How can Christian faith continue to announce such a prospect in the world after Auschwitz, after Hiroshima? Especially when this faith does not close its eyes to death and decay, to leukemia and mass murder by napalm, but dares to proclaim the hope of life and liberty from the perspective of one dead on a cross!

The scandal remains, today as ever. Because it is rooted in man's disbelief in himself and in the meaning of historical existence, it is more acute today than ever before.

This means that there is no easy transition from the world's questions to the gospel's answers (or its questions!). We have indeed come to the end of the age of rationality. But that does not mean that we are able to set aside all the questions, the doubt, and the skepticism which that age raised for faith, and embrace God and meaning unquestioningly. None of us is able to do that. Clearly enough, human reason, as envisaged by the Enlightenment, has failed as a way of salvation. But its failure as a way of salvation does not imply that the problems it raised for all religious ways of salvation have been rendered null and void. The questions of Hume and Voltaire, of Rousseau and Feuerbach, of Thomas Hardy and all the others remain. They all contribute to the form in which the scandal of the gospel presents itself to us today. Therefore we should not expect anyone to find it easier to accept Jesus Christ just because other gospels, and notably the world's own do-it-yourself gospel, have become incredible. The scandal that anchors faith in history, like a tree or a cross planted in the earth, remains.

But False Scandals Are Fewer

Nevertheless it is true that in our time many of what Bultmann called the "false scandals" have been removed.

A false scandal is something that *seems* to get in the way of belief, but in reality only serves to camouflage the real scandal. Some aspect of belief, actual or alleged, becomes a barrier to serious confrontation with the heart of the gospel itself. For example, people say that they cannot accept Christianity because it requires belief in the virgin birth or in the physical resurrection. Or they find intellectual difficulties concerning the question of God's existence. These are not unimportant aspects of Christian faith, but neither are they anything like the core of it. The core is far more immediate, more personal. It has to do with my life, with the lives of my loved ones, my species, our world. It puts me on the spot. It cuts to the quick.

Unlike the authentic scandal, the false *skandalon* keeps the whole thing at arm's length. It can be a matter for objective discussion: Does God exist? Could a child be born of a virgin?—a *God*-child? Did the body of Jesus actually come to life again?

"How" questions

I remember all those nice problems we used to indulge in when I was a student in the university. They seem so remote now—and so contrived. Those endless debates about science and religion, creation versus evolution, reason and faith. We used to be quite elated whenever we discovered a scientist who believed in God, or at least didn't disbelieve. We thought it was terribly important, a sort of event, when one of them would sit down with a group of Christian students and quietly convey the impression that, yes, he too was a searcher after the Absolute.

That has changed. I don't mean that more scientists and other intellectuals are now ready to believe in God. Rather, what has changed is the consistent atmosphere of quiet objectivity and noninvolvement. A significant minority within the universities and elsewhere have been shocked out of their nicely objectified worlds. They have looked through their microscopes and found the enemy: themselves. Demographers, suddenly conscious of the silent explosion in world population, have been driven to ask the apocalyptic question, "Can man *survive?*" Sociologists and historians, coming out of their borrowed value-free world view, have echoed,

"Well, can *man* survive?" Many for whom the world of
pure research was to have been so dispassionate, a guarantee against commitment, have become committed in
spite of themselves. Academic apathy has given way to
anxious concern. Or let us call it, with Tillich, "ultimate concern."

This "ultimate concern" on the part of many sensitive intellectuals and ordinary mortals today has dis-
pelled a good deal of the atmosphere in which false
scandals could thrive. The false scandal thrives only
where people can still maintain the facade of noninvolvement. In fact, that is its real function: to help to
maintain that removedness, that insulation against life's
real stumbling blocks. It is Françoise Sagan crooning
with suave nonchalance: "God? I never think of it."
Human beings who are ultimately concerned are not
very good candidates for this nonchalance. "God?" asks
one of the characters in Beckett's play *Endgame*—"God?
He doesn't exist. The bastard!"[12] For Beckett, the false
scandal has been removed: he confronts the stumbling
block head on.

There probably aren't many today for whom the
question of God is as real as it is for Beckett. But there
are many, a great many, who manifest ultimate concern. The object of their ultimate concern is man. That
is precisely why the Christian, who professes belief in
a God who also seems to have the world of man as his
ultimate concern, can find in these persons a point of
meeting that is beyond the quasi-seriousness of the false
scandal. To me it is far more significant that today I
meet many who are ultimately concerned about man
than that yesterday I met some who were intellectually
curious about God.

Encounter point

Wherever Christians can make their own ultimate concern for the world and mankind real, in word and deed, they can expect to encounter many others who have been moved to this same compassion. Many of those others will be strange bedfellows indeed. But that doesn't matter. We meet, not as people bound together by ideologies or doctrines, but as those who are vigilant for man and earth. The scandal of faith, including the scandal of particularity, is not removed. We are not meeting for the same reasons, with identical hopes and fears. We do not even have the same programs. But a great deal of the bric-a-brac that formerly prevented us from meeting at all has been removed. At least we can meet around a point of ultimate concern.

The condition for the meeting, however, rests largely with the Christians. False scandals are not only barriers that the world throws up, to protect itself from hearing the Word of the cross. Christians, too, from their side, are notorious for perpetuating the false *skandalon*. From the beginning, we Christians have used penultimate and secondary concerns of faith to protect ourselves from dialogue with the world. We can only expect to meet the others who are vigilant for man if we dispense altogether with this resort to the false scandal. To comprehend fully what that would mean, it is necessary to grasp that our most treasured theological truths frequently become the very stuff out of which the false scandal is fashioned. For most of those with whom we could engage in meaningful exchange today, every aspect of faith will be false scandal if it keeps us from communicating to them that *our* ultimate concern, too, is man and earth.

In his famous poem *Abou Ben Adhem*, Leigh Hunt

found the pagan man Abou acceptable to God because
he loved his fellowmen. If "pagan" men sometimes find
Christians credible in the world today, it is for the same
reason. They believe that those Christians do, after all,
love their fellowmen.

❦ 2 ❧

SOME SPECIFIC POINTS OF MEETING

(concern)
Love Is Not Enough!

It is not adequate, however, to leave the matter at
that. Love for mankind, ultimate concern for the race
and the planet—this, I think, is what knits together
many Christians and non-Christians today, and makes
it possible for the latter to discern a new sort of reality
in the Christian gospel. Although that is the necessary
condition for openness, mutuality of love and concern
could not of itself sustain the encounter. For non-faith
to be impelled to continue the dialogue with faith, there
must be quite specific points at which they are able to
talk with each other. More than that, non-faith must be
able to trust that faith can somehow illuminate their
mutual concerns.

Quite concretely this means that a certain responsibility to become newly articulate is placed on Christians who grasp the potential significance of this dialogue. It is not enough just to love man and the world.
Deeds of love there must be. But there must also be
words. And I don't mean merely words of concern, dec-
larations of solidarity. In respect to solidarity, deeds
always speak louder than words. What you do during

an election campaign speaks more loudly of your solidarity with mankind than sermons or speeches at the Rotary Club!

By the need for words, I refer, rather, to a theological necessity. Christians who feel, and by their deeds manifest, solidarity with the world of man need to become freshly immersed in the struggle of faith itself. They themselves have to become the place where the gospel is confronted by the anxious questions of the age: e.g., "Can the world be saved?" But not merely confronted by such questions as if they were the old, predictably religious questions. It is true that the world can even put its questions in quite traditional religious terms. But they mean something quite different from what our grandfathers meant when they asked the same questions at their revival meetings. Questions such as "Can the world be saved?" incorporate today a great many dimensions that our grandfathers never dreamed of. On the whole, Christians have a very poor grasp of those dimensions.

That must be changed. What Nicodemus wants to know when he comes to you by night is not whether you share his concern. The fact that you were there in the night, that he came to you at all, indicates that he thinks you do share his concern. He wants to know whether you can shed any light on his concern. At least, can you help him to understand what is wrong? If you are able to provide even a minimum of insight into the malaise of the epoch, he may go on to inquire about the alternative you try to pursue beyond this present way of death. He will always be grateful for your support; but what he wants and needs is more than support. There may never before have been a time in history when it was so important for Christians to be theologically and intellectually alive.

To illustrate: I shall never forget what was asked of me when I first joined the company of scientists, social scientists, and others who were planning the interdisciplinary course to which I referred earlier. This course was inspired by the manifold crisis of the environment. A geographer looked at me with evident interest in my presence at the planning session. There was a hint of overt suspicion in his glance. "And what do you think *you* can contribute to the course?" he asked gently but firmly. My concern and my solidarity, without which I should not have been asked to participate in this experiment, were not sufficient. I had to be prepared to contribute something. Like the others on the teaching committee, I was expected from my discipline, Christian theology, to illuminate the problematic indicated in the title of the course: "Man and the Biosphere."

Six years later I have to confess that I had to learn from others what questions to tackle, where I could best make my contribution.

For the most part, I think, Christians are so demoralized, so convinced that they have nothing to contribute to the world's discussion of its life and death, that they do their best to avoid these encounters. If they are thrust into situations where they cannot remain safely silent, they do their best to avoid speaking straightforwardly as Christians. They quote those authorities they think the world honors—sometimes with unfortunate results. If the subject is human sexuality, they let Freud or David West or someone else do their analysis for them. Here and there a theological decoration is tacked on. If it's technology, they listen with special care to

people such as Robert Theobald or perhaps Lewis
Mumford or Marshall McLuhan. Theodore Roszak's
book on the counter culture enabled Christians to form
an opinion about hippies and others.[13] Sometimes, if
they are quite intrepid, Christians allow themselves the
risk of saying something, as Christians, by way of answer to these problems—once they have allowed the
experts to define the questions. It rarely occurs to them
—especially if they are working in committees—that
they may even be able to bring some insight to the
analysis of the problem. They are almost totally convinced that these matters are too deep for them or, at
least, are beyond their field of competency.

Thus it is not unusual today to discover secular inves-
tigators in every field of human endeavor who pick up
various things out of the Judeo-Christian tradition to
use in their own attempts to understand the modern
world. One is tempted to say that when the Christians
are silent, the very stones will cry out. Freud never
really acknowledged the Biblical sources of many of his
best ideas, for example, the so-called "death wish." And
Karl Marx rather gave the impression that he had per-
sonally invented the idea of a meaningful goal in history. But many contemporary seers are quoting the
Bible forthrightly, and openly drawing on the tradition
of Jerusalem for wisdom.

Thus we see that men of the world are finding new
interests and a new sense of reality in Biblical faith. We
now turn to examine some of the specific points in
which the dialogue between faith and non-faith can
take place.

\# 1   *"Whatever Became of Sin?"*

"Whatever became of sin?" asks the world-renowned scientist of the human psyche, Karl Menninger. He dares to use *that* word! When Reinhold Niebuhr and the others presumed to reintroduce that word into the theological dialogue earlier in this century, many liberal Christians were shocked and incensed. They could only regard Niebuhr and his ilk as untimely pessimists, or new exponents of an old orthodoxy that had long since been relegated to the theological garbage heap. Now we have a secular man, representative of a secular discipline, asking about his world in terms of "sin."

In the initial chapter of the recent book that puts this question as its title, Dr. Menninger recounts the following incident:

> On a sunny day in September, 1972, a stern-faced, plainly dressed man could be seen standing still on a street corner in the busy Chicago Loop. As pedestrians hurried by on their way to lunch or business, he would solemnly lift his right arm, and pointing to the person nearest him, intone loudly the single word, "GUILTY!"
>
> Then, without any change of expression, he would resume his stiff stance for a few moments before repeating the gesture. Then again, the inexorable raising of his arm, the pointing, and the solemn pronouncing of the one word "GUILTY!"[14]

With this provocative beginning, Menninger goes on to write the sort of historical synopsis of Western civilization that most intellectuals two decades ago would have found unthinkable, Spengler and others notwithstanding. It is a story of failure and regress. It passes through various stages of our development, which we are accustomed to regard as a ladder leading ever upward to the light. Unimpressed by the Enlightenment, it comes at last to our own contemporary North American scene:

> Noisy display enticed people in less prosperous countries to rush to our shores and join in the great grab. These newcomers were exploited in order to produce more and more "gross national products" and electrical energy. We dammed up more and more rivers and gouged out more coal and smashed down more forests. Our population increased—too much. Our traffic increased—much too much. Everything was "going great"—but too much.
>
> Suddenly we awoke from our pleasant dreams with a fearful realization that *something was wrong.*[15]

In the concluding statement of the book, Menninger—the scientist—quotes with approval the following words of Arnold Toynbee:

> Science has never superseded religion, and it is my expectation that it never will supersede it. . . . Science has also begun to find out how to cure psychic sickness. So far, however, science has shown no signs that it is going to be able to cope with man's most serious problems. It has not been able to do anything to cure man of his sinfulness and his sense of insecurity, or to avert the painfulness of failure and the dread of death. Above all, it has not helped him to break out of the prison of his inborn self-centeredness into communion or union with some reality that is greater, more important, more valuable, and more lasting than the individual himself.
>
> I am convinced, myself, that man's fundamental problem is his egocentricity.[16]

Not only is Karl Menninger prepared to discuss this world (for 250 pages) under the rubric of this ancient concept of sin, but he has a few words for those to whose vocabulary this word is supposed in particular to belong:

> Egocentricity is one name for it. Selfishness, narcissism, pride, and other terms have also been used. But neither the clergy nor the behavioral scientists, including psychiatrists, have made it an issue. The popular leaning is away from notions of guilt and morality. . . .
>
> A trumpet call like that of Toynbee's phrase compels one to stop and reflect. We know that the principal leadership in the morality realm should be the clergy's [Strange, how this idea persists!], but they seem to minimize their great traditional and historical opportunity to preach, to prophesy, to speak out. . . .
>
> Some clergymen prefer pastoral counseling of individuals to the pulpit function. But the latter is a greater opportunity to prevent some of the accumulated misapprehensions, guilt, aggressive action, and other roots of later mental suffering and mental disease.
>
> How? Preach! Tell it like it is. Say it from the pulpit. Cry it from the housetops.
>
> What shall we cry?
>
> Cry comfort, cry repentance, cry hope. Because *recognition of our part in the world transgression is the only remaining hope.*[17]

One suspects that what Menninger means by the clergy's negligence of sin is not mere negligence of the word as such. God knows that one hears it often enough, especially from the ecclesiastical right wing. What he means, I think, is our apparent inability to apply the insights that derive from this Hebraic concept imaginatively to our own experience as a people.

There could be no better illustration of the imaginative application of Biblical understanding of sin to our contemporary situation than is contained in that final sentence of the last quotation: "Because recognition of our part in the world transgression is the only remaining hope." It would be difficult to discover a more insightful grasp of the gospel's understanding of the reality of sin.

Awareness of the Demonic

Not only is it possible to find people of the world who know how to use the word "sin" imaginatively today but there is also a growing awareness of the demonic character of evil.

This is a strange phenomenon in a society that was supposed to have become entirely secular, that was supposed to have passed quite beyond the childish habit of attributing good and evil, fortune and misfortune, joy and sorrow to transcendent causes. Today there is considerable justification for thinking that we have more in common with the Middle Ages than with the age of reason. Nowhere is this more in evidence than in the interest of a great cross section of society in the demonic.

Record attendances are reported by theaters across the continent showing *The Exorcist*. The pursuit of the world of darkness is manifested in every form, from the most serious worship of Satan to the apparently innocent captivation of the bourgeois household by television shows such as *Bewitched*.

Once again, however, I want to avoid these more popular or occult manifestations of contemporary man's openness to specific points of Biblical faith. To illustrate the awareness of the demonic, I will turn to something undoubtedly more subtle—but also more rudimentary—namely, the growing awareness on the part of many people today that what we call "technology" is a *power.* It is a power that transcends both the individual and the collective will of man. By its increasingly efficient manipulation of nature, it is almost inevitably destructive of human life and society.

As the Canadian political philosopher George Grant has demonstrated with impeccable logic, the manipulation of nature, which is the basis and aim of the technocratic mind-set, must finally mean the manipulation of *human* nature.[18] In his cool way B. F. Skinner has proposed that we can no longer afford "freedom and dignity."[19] He is not the monster he is sometimes made out to be. His proposal is the logical consequence of a mental construct that from the outset of the modern epoch set itself to control nature.

This determination to master nature has an even more interesting aspect. What gives it its metaphysical dimension and renders the struggle as having demonic proportions is that nature is looked upon as the enemy. "Confront it with audacity!" cries Thomas Hobbes, one of the earlier formulators of this mind-set.[20] Since the public has become aware of the ecological crisis, everybody has disdained this kind of language. Even the Ford Motor Company and the other great technocratic empires of industry have become friends and lovers of nature. But we should not be fooled by this protestation. The economic and psychic foundation of our society is still the absolute mastery of nature. It is better to trust the earlier statements of the technocrats than those found in present advertisements and elsewhere. "Nature is the enemy; she must be brought to her knees!" exclaims the narrator of a public relations film produced about a decade ago by a large hydroelectric concern. And not incidentally, the rest of the narration was positively studded with quotations from the Scriptures!

In the process of conquering nature, modern man neglected to notice that he himself was a segment of what he wanted to control. This neglect is partly to be explained on the basis of an earlier assumption, which for a long time he was able to maintain, that he himself transcended nature almost infinitely. The natural sciences, the work of Darwin and others, has had a contrary effect. Man is set solidly and exclusively within the natural universe: a species among species, a species that can disappear, just as the dinosaurs disappeared. Thus, increasingly, man has lost his sense of transcendence and the sense of purpose that went with it. The crowning irony is that this has happened just at the point where his technological apparatus, by which he thought to conquer nature, has become almost *sui generis*. Without strong, operative goals born of the sense of human dignity and purpose, the means have become ends in themselves. Hence, what began as a Promethean conquest of nature has ended in the subjugation of man to the very processes he set in motion. He is "hoist with his own petard," as the old expression phrased it.

Those who have understood the technocratic mentality in demonic terms, that is, in the sense of a transcendent evil, have done so because they sense the threat to man that is implicit in modern technique. Many critics of technologism whose criticisms are still pertinent offered them long before our own time. There is, in fact, a long and impressive history of struggle against "the machine" on the part of those who were vigilant for man. It is there in Blake, in Dickens, in Gerhart Hauptmann's *The Weavers*, in Rice's *The Adding Machine*. At the beginning of the nineteenth century it was publicly demonstrated in the pathetic struggle of the Luddites— people I was taught in public school to regard as madmen, but about whom many of my contemporaries are now saying very different things. Somebody even called them the last of the human beings.

What makes it necessary for us to take with utter seriousness the discussion of technology as a power alien to true humanity, however, is not the protest against "the machine" as such. The machine, as perceptive contemporary critics have understood better than their forerunners in this protest, is merely "symptomatic" (Ellul) of the problem. The machine is not the cause but an effect. What is at issue is the mechanization and manipulation of existence.

It is in such terms that Heidegger, for example, discusses the technocratic mentality.[21] So does Josef Pieper, the German philosopher of culture.[22] So do novelists such as Tolkien, Bradbury, Huxley, and Orwell. The dimension of transcendent evil is present in many contemporary sociological analyses as well. Philip Slater's *The Pursuit of Loneliness*[23] was an imaginative attempt to present the Bohemian wing of the counter culture as a reaction against the technocratic manipulation of human life.

One of the most comprehensive studies of this subject to date has been that of the Christian lay theologian and sociologist Jacques Ellul. Since I am attempting here to provide instances of nonreligious analyses that have found it necessary to reach again for the category of transcendent evil to explain this phenomenon, Ellul may seem out of context. I include him, however, because he provides evidence of the point I am endeavoring to make, only from a different angle. The interesting fact about his book *The Technological Society*[24] is that still today many who make most use of it do not know that it is the work of a Christian theologian. At the same time, those who know Ellul's other works, and something of the tradition of Augustine, Calvin, and Karl Barth, realize that this book could not have been written apart from that point of departure. This indicates from another perspective the openness of the non-Christian, nonreligious world to Christian analysis imaginatively done.

While discursive treatments of the technological society such as those of Ellul, George Grant, and Philip Slater are necessary, I sometimes feel that a better entrée into the subject is provided by the arts. Perhaps a mystery as deep as the power of "La Technique" in our lives can only be portrayed and grasped symbolically.

One who understands this power well and is able to communicate his understanding to thousands, especially to the young, is the storyteller Kurt Vonnegut, Jr. Serious authors and readers often dismiss Vonnegut as a writer of science fiction or black humor. What he seems to me to grasp better than most of those who comment on technology, however, is just this dimension we are calling here the demonic. In other words, he understands intuitively the sort of thing that Rubem Alves means when he writes, "The idea of the neutrality of science and technology is no longer tenable."[25]

But before I document that from Vonnegut's writings, let me observe something about us Christians. Menninger says we have stopped talking convincingly of sin. It could be claimed with at least equal validity that we have also stopped talking with imagination about the demonic. There is no better evidence of this than that provided in our usual pronouncements on technology.

Alves seems to be one of the very few contemporary Christians who understands that technology is a power —a means that has taken on the function of an end. On the whole, Christians approach the discussion of the technological society in the naïve assumption that technology is neutral. This attitude, which is reproduced in nearly every corporate ecclesiastical or ecumenical statement as well as from pulpits, can be represented as follows: "Technology is with us to stay; it can be used by us for great evil or great good; let us by all means use it for great good."

Official Marxism, incidentally, approaches the subject in the same way, and assumes that if only the world were ruled by Marxist principles and not by technocratic capitalists, there would be no problem. This assumption is seriously belied by the realities of industrial despoliation of the environment in Communist lands, to say nothing of the manipulation of man in those same societies.[26]

The assumption that technology is merely neutral is naïve. It disregards not only the data of technocratic manipulation but also something far more rudimentary. It disregards the whole tragic dimension of human existence, including the fact that man constantly falls prey to powers stronger than himself. There may be some excuse for this naïveté in doctrinaire Marxism, which has steadfastly refused to confront all the evidence the twentieth century has thrown up. But surely there is no excuse for Christians to misunderstand this tragic dimension. One of the most conspicuous marks of contemporary Christian mediocrity is this: at a time when worldly men are exploring the great controlling forces of their age along the lines of transcendent evil, Christians mostly mouth the platitudes of the eighteenth and nineteenth centuries, saying that we must decide to use these forces for good ends. Have we lost all touch with what Paul meant by "principalities and powers"?

At a conference of the World Council of Churches in France in 1973 on the topic "Technology and the Quality of Life" I sat transfixed as an American technocrat spoke about the future. He had oversight of all air traffic in the United States. In the course of his address he stated, quite dispassionately, that it was totally unthinkable that rail and other public ground transportation might be increased on this continent, and air traffic lessened. Someone raised a question about that in view of the energy crisis. The speaker became more passionate: "Look!" he exclaimed, somewhat exasperated. "I can't tell you how it *ought to* be, I can only tell you how it *is* . . . and *will be!*"

No Christian present objected, in spite of the fact that the almost unanimous assumption of the conference—that technology is neutral and should be used for good—ought to have sent every man to his feet protesting. The point is, the technocrat was telling the truth. He could *not* tell us how it should be; he could *not* cause

the "is" and the "will be" to be altered by an "ought to
be." He could only serve the process. As Alves has
written:

> "The more things change the more they remain the same."
> One can change at will those who seem to be in power and
> shift from one party to another. It makes no difference.
> Because those who seem to be in charge are not really in
> charge. They are nothing more than transistors in a net-
> work of power, executives plugged into a system. And
> ultimately it is the system that programs the course of
> operations. Individuals are expendable, disposable. Paul
> already knew this political reality better than we. "For our
> fight is not against human foes, but against cosmic powers,
> against [the] authorities and potentates of this dark world,
> against the superhuman forces of evil in the heavens."
> (Eph. 6:12.)[27]

To return to Vonnegut—he also knows. In his own,
sometimes peculiar way he knows that technology is a
power under whose influence man has fallen—at first as
a matter of decision, perhaps, but increasingly because
he was not in a position to make decisions anymore.
Vonnegut understands that it is almost impossible—
perhaps it will really prove impossible—for Western
man to overcome the power of the technocratic world
view to which he submitted long ago, and of which he
has become the huckster throughout the world. Perhaps he is driven by a collective death wish and will not
be satisfied until he has relinquished the last vestiges of
his freedom and dignity to the efficient system.

This dreadful prospect informs a parable that Vonnegut tells in his book *The Sirens of Titan*. A robot from
a far-off planet, Tralfamadore, explains the fate of certain beings on his planet long ago. In the distant past,

he recounts, Tralfamadore had supported beings "who weren't anything like machines": "They weren't dependable. They weren't efficient. They weren't predictable. They weren't durable." These strange beings had the fixed notion that whatever existed must have some "purpose." Moreover, they insisted, some "purposes" are weightier than others.

And yet, every time these beings discovered something that could be regarded as a raison d'être, they quickly became disenchanted with it: it seemed to them "so low." Instead of giving themselves over to such an ignoble goal, they would invent a machine to fulfill that particular end.

Soon, machines had been created that could service not only the lower but also the higher functions; and they "did everything so expertly" that they were at last charged with the task of uncovering what the "highest purpose" of the strange, nonmechanical beings might be.

"The machines," according to the robot's account, "reported in all honesty that the creatures couldn't really be said to have any purpose at all.

"The creatures thereupon began slaying each other, because they hated purposeless things above all else." But it immediately became apparent that they weren't even very adept at killing. Consequently that task, too, was given over to the machines. "And the machines finished up the job in less time than it takes to say 'Tralfamadore.' "[28]

Beneath the ironic humor of this parable are depths of understanding that surpass the imagining of most professional theologians and ministers. One has only to reflect a little on the connection that the parable makes between the discovery of purposelessness and war. "Nothing," writes Jacques Ellul, "equals the perfection of our war machines."[29] And Nietzsche, as if he had been writing a philosophic punch line for Vonnegut's story, said that man's will to power is so vast that when he finds there is nothing left to will, he will will . . . nothing.[30]

The demonic is always associated with the pursuit of oblivion, a hankering after nothingness. The point at which technology took a turn toward the demonic was where modern man began to suspect that he had no purpose; that the universe was quite "indifferent" (Camus) to his existence. But the condition for making technology a demonic pursuit was laid long before that. It originated with man's dissatisfaction with the purposes that *were* discovered for him—namely, his dissatisfaction with his own humanity, his own creatureliness, and his consequent futile search for "higher purposes." And that, if we can again make the reference to our own Christian sources, is as old as Adam!

#3

The Sense of an Ending

A third and closely related point where one observes today a new openness to the story that Christians tell is what may be called the sense of an ending.

When we were children growing up in a small Ontario village, there was an announcement on the radio one day that a certain religious group was predicting the end of the world for the very next day. We thought that a great joke, but we entered into the spirit of the thing. We spent all that day—the last day of history!—having a whale of a time. It was winter, so our Dionysian orgy expressed itself as a form of abandonment to the snow. By evening we were so wet with slush that our mothers almost made the prediction come true, at least for us!

The point is that in that context we simply couldn't take such an idea to heart—even though it was, perhaps, the year 1938 or 1939. Archbishop Temple was wondering whether it might not have been better to pursue a religion of redemption, and across the Atlantic another figure was already instituting something closely related to Nietzsche's statement about willing nothing.

Today the apocalyptic seems far more existential. It often produces the same kind of abandon—not with the Dionysian snow so much as with "grass" and other things. But beneath the abandon there is a great melancholy, an emotion not at all like the hilarity we children of that long-ago world found in the snow. Much of today's hilarity is counterfeit.

Not many people actually assign a date for the end of the world. It isn't necessary. The sense of an ending is more real to us now than it was during those times when dates were given out. It is not only a feature but is the *characteristic* feature of our society. The omega factor hangs over the heads of not only a few eccentric artists and religious extremists; it is ubiquitous. It is present in the air we breathe. As Norman Mailer has written of our century:

> A century devoted to the rationality of technique was also a century so irrational as to open in every mind the real possibility of global destruction. It was the first century in history which presented to sane and sober minds the fair chance that the century might not reach the end of its span.[31]

One of the "sane and sober minds" quite conscious of this apocalyptic factor is the great scientist René Dubos. He has written:

> There is perhaps some symbolism, as yet incompletely deciphered, in the visions that St. John the Divine had on the island of Patmos. The first horsemen of the Apocalypse that he saw were Famine and Pestilence. Then another was sent by the angered Deity. After the fifth angel had sounded his trumpet he opened the bottomless pit and "there arose a smoke out of the pit, as the smoke of a great furnace; and the sun and the air were darkened by reason of the smoke of the pit." And out of the bottomless pit there came the scorpions that did not kill men but tormented them for five months before final destruction came "by the fire, and by the smoke, and by the brimstone." The time of fulfillment of the Apocalypse may not be far off.[32]

Ernst Käsemann has presented the provocative thesis that "apocalyptic is the mother of Christian theology."[33] This is not the place to debate that thesis. But it is certainly true that the earliest Christians lived with the prospect of an omega. Indeed, they interpreted their whole life in terms of it. For them, the end was the beginning; the omega they looked for contained within it a redemptive alpha.

Contemporary man does not count on that possibility. For him, the end, whether "bang" or "whimper" (Eliot), is more threat than promise. Yet the very sense of an ending links contemporary man with Christianity in provocative ways. There is a real sense in which a Christian today, if he is sufficiently aware of the apocalyptic origins and presuppositions of his own believing, can enter into immediate dialogue with men who express opinions such as those of Mailer and Dubos.

Those who must be left out of the dialogue are Christians who are either too frightened or too apathetic to come to grips with the omega in our own midst. Unfortunately they frequently just get in the way of the dialogue. To them, this question of Karl Jaspers needs to be addressed:

> One is tempted to ask . . . : If the first Christians believed in the end of the world, if they were sure of it even though they did not know, even though they were in fact, mistaken—do we today, who know the fact, have to believe it as well, to accept its reality, and to make it a factor in our way of life?[34]

The Search for a Way Into the Future

So far, I have been discussing points of contact with the world that are in a specific sense related to the Christian analysis of the human predicament: sin, the demonic, the sense of an ending. But it would be a mistake to think that it is only in terms of the analysis of the problem that there can be meaningful dialogue between faith and committed non-faith today.

It is somehow natural that the most *obvious* points of meeting should be these predicamental ones. For as a people we have become aware that we are in a state of predicament. For us in North America it is the first time that this sense has gripped us deeply and universally.

Once a people begins to express doubt about its future, it begins at the same time to be open to alternatives to the way of life that has heretofore impelled it. So on every hand today we hear the cry that unless we can develop a completely new life-style, unless we can find new values, we are doomed. This insistent theme car-

ries not only a negative assessment of the way of life we
have followed but a positive openness to something
else.

The complicating factor for Christians who sense
this casting about for new ways, new values and life-
styles on the part of many of their nonreligious neighbors, is that few of them are ever attracted to Christianity in this search. Certainly not to the Christianity of
our so-called major denominations. That type of Christianity does not strike them as anything like an *alternative* to what we already have. On the contrary, for the
most part they see it as a central feature of what we
have. Moreover, it is identified with what is *wrong* with
what we have! Once more we find ourselves at the core
of the problem that this study seeks to investigate. The
sad thing is that there are good reasons why so many
can only see Christianity as part of the Establishment,
the way of life which has led us to this precipice. We
shall return to that later.

For the present, we may simply recognize that there
are points at which the human, not-overtly-religious
search for a way into the future coincides with basic
Christian convictions. Where those convictions are able
to break free of their official connections, where Christians are able to make themselves credible in human
ways, the human search for a future is strangely parallel
at many points. Often the parallel surprises both par-
ties, Christians and non-Christians alike.

According to Theodore Roszak, the parallel is seen in
the counter culture, although Christians are often the
last to see any connection!

The Christian example is one that many of the hip young are quick to invoke, perhaps with more appropriateness than many of their critics may recognize. Hopelessly estranged by ethos and social class from the official culture, the primitive Christian community awkwardly fashioned out of Judaism and the mystery cults a minority culture that could not but seem an absurdity to Greco-Roman orthodoxy. But the absurdity, far from being felt as a disgrace, became a banner of the community.

Then Roszak quotes Paul's words about the foolishness of the cross, and comments: "It is a familiar passage from what is now an oppressively respectable source."[35]

I want to discuss three points at which the contemporary search for alternatives touches upon basic Christian beliefs regarding the life to which mankind is called. To reiterate: I do not regard these points of contact as constituting an immediate link between faith and non-faith. The scandal of the cross remains, that is, the insistence that the "abundant life" can be gained only as the gift of God, given only at the point of death with the one "true man." These points of meeting represent, however, places where now and then, here and there, the gospel possesses potential reality and depth for many outside the faith.

The Search for a New Relation to Nature

One such point of meeting concerns the attempt of many today to find a new way of being vis-à-vis nature.

"I am pessimistic about the human race," wrote Rachel Carson several years ago in her book *Silent Spring,* because it is too ingenious for its own good. Our approach to nature is to beat it into submission. We would stand a better chance of survival if we accommodated ourselves to this planet and viewed it appreciatively, instead of skeptically and dictatorially.[36]

When Rachel Carson wrote these words many intelligent people thought her something of a crank. Since then her advance warning about the deterioration of the natural environment has been validated many times over.

Many today wonder how we can learn to live with nature without destroying it, and ourselves with it. In their search for a new way, they also ask about the historic roots of the old. It is a shaming, damning testimony to the church's identification with the spirit of industrial society, that many who ask about these historic roots point an accusing finger squarely at the Judeo-Christian tradition.

Thus the British ecologist Frank Fraser Darling, in his 1969 Reith Lectures, stated:

Our Greek derivation in Western civilization gave us the reason which has guided our science, but the Judaic-Christian background gave us a man-centred world. Our technology is a monument to the belief that Jehovah created us in his image, a belief which of course had to be put that way to express the truth that man created Jehovah in *his* own image. The resources of the planet were for man, without a doubt. They could have no higher end than to serve man at the behest of Jehovah. There could be no doubt about the rightness of technology.[37]

A similar charge, which has achieved almost the status of a papal encyclical among many environmentalists—one editor introduces it as "perhaps a classic in its own right"[38]—is that of the historian Lynn White, Jr. In his essay "The Historical Roots of Our Ecologic Crisis," Professor White lays the blame for the environmental crisis on the doorstep of Biblical religion, with its ideas of man's transcendence of nature and his divine prerogative to master it:

> We would seem to be headed towards conclusions unpalatable to many Christians. Since both *science* and *technology* are blessed words in our contemporary vocabulary, some may be happy at the notions, first, that viewed historically, modern science is an extrapolation of natural theology and, second, that modern technology is at least partly to be explained as an Occidental, voluntarist realization of the Christian dogma of man's transcendence of, and rightful mastery over, nature. But, as we now recognize, somewhat over a century ago science and technology—hitherto quite separate activities—joined to give mankind powers which, to judge by many of the ecologic effects, are out of control. If so, Christianity bears a huge burden of guilt.[39]

It can be pointed out without difficulty that White's argument is oversimplified and misleading. Many have challenged it. This should not, however, insulate Christians against the judgment hidden in this accusation. The fact is, whatever the Biblical conception of man's relation to nature, Christianity, at least from the sixteenth century on, aligned itself squarely with that spirit which gave rise to the age of science and eventually to the industrial revolution. The Luddites, to whom I have already made passing reference, for their crime of attacking the sacred (and privately owned!) machines of man, were told by a Christian judge that

before they were hanged they should go out and make
their peace with the Christian God:

> Give yourselves up to the pious admonitions of the rever-
> end Clergyman, whose office it will be to prepare you for
> your awful change; and God grant, that, worthily lament-
> ing your sins, and acknowledging your wretchedness, you
> may obtain of the God of all mercy perfect remission and
> forgiveness.[40]

In relation to the whole question of man and nature,
Christianity faces today a tremendous apologetic task.
For it has allowed one side of the Biblical dialectic
(man's transcendence of and authority within nature)
to outshadow altogether the other side (man's involvement within and responsibility for nature).

In the face of this complicity of Christianity in the of-
fenses of industrial and post-industrial society, it is a wonder that anyone finds in Christianity any potential for
developing a new understanding of the relation between
man and nature. In fact, very few non-Christians do.

But Christians who have their ears to the ground, and
who are not willing to let the Christian faith be circumscribed by ecclesiastical practice over the past few centuries, can hear familiar things in the gropings of secular men for new ways of relating to their environment.
They are calling for a man who sees himself, not as the
master of the universe with no one to answer to, but as
participant in a complex ecological cycle in which he
will be sustained only so long as he acts responsibly to
sustain the others. They want a man who is not lord but
only steward of creation; a man who receives his daily
bread, though he did not cause the grain to grow; a man
who is not permitted to hoard up manna, in his in-

security and greed, at the expense of other men and of creatures committed to man's keeping; a man who recognizes the limits of his creaturehood and who looks for his possibilities *within* those limits.

Hence many of the pronouncements of ecological, economic, and scientific groups today (such as the Club of Rome's *Limits to Growth*[41]) sound a little like the Sermon on the Mount. The German chemist Klaus Müller, of Braunschweig, has said in his best-selling study of our situation: We have come to the place in human experience where the Sermon on the Mount must become a political reality, or else we will perish.[42]

The Search for World Brotherhood

A second point at which the Christian should be able to enter into constructive dialogue with the human search for an alternative way is the attempt to find world community. Not only is it essential for mankind to discern a new mode of being vis-à-vis the natural environment; it is equally essential that we find a new way of being with our fellowmen.

This theme is—rather, is reputed to be!—so familiar to all of us in North America that it seems to need no elaboration. Are not we all staunch supporters of the United Nations? Are not all Americans and Canadians true internationalists? Do not we Christians pray without ceasing for world brotherhood, and send off money, personnel, and bales of goods to prove that we mean it?

Listen to these words from the concluding chapter of a compelling study by Barbara Ward and René Dubos, two of the world's most brilliant and committed scientists, one an economist, the other a biologist:

Our new knowledge of our planetary interdependence demands that the functions [of our societies] are now seen to be world-wide and supported with as rational a concept as self-interest. Governments have already paid lip-service to such a view of the world by setting up the whole variety of United Nations agencies whose duty it is to elaborate world-wide strategies. But the idea of authority and energy and resources to support their policies seems strange, visionary and Utopian at present, simply because world institutions are not backed by any sense of planetary community and commitment. Indeed, the whole idea of operating effectively at the world level still seems in some way peculiar and unlikely. The planet is not yet a centre of rational loyalty for all mankind.[43]

In order to grasp the full significance of this statement, we should reflect that it is the conclusion of a report, commissioned by the Secretary General of the United Nations Conference on the Human Environment, presented in the English language to the English-speaking world. Its implied skepticism does not stem from a lack of trust in the "underdeveloped" peoples. It stems from a terrible uncertainty about the "privileged." It concludes that among us—the enlightened, literate, globe-trotting, and largely Christian peoples of the English-speaking nations—unfortunately there is not yet a sufficient "sense of planetary consciousness" or "loyalty for all mankind" to make such a thing as the United Nations actually work.

For nearly two thousand years, Christians have been reading the prayer of Jesus "that all may be one," not to mention countless other Biblical testimonies to this sought-for unity. But none of this apparently has prepared the ground for serious international commitment. We still receive the idea of human brotherhood as purely utopian and visionary.

As in the case of the relation between man and nature, it is once again an almost overwhelming condemnation of Christianity that it has had so little real influence on the question of world unity. It speaks volumes about the character of the Christian religion as a *Western* establishment. The truth is that we could not maintain sufficient distinction from the cultures of our individual Western nations to convince even our own people, let alone those of non-Western lands, that Jesus Christ's love and Lordship transcends national boundaries. Not only did we carry Western imperialism in government and culture with us into foreign lands, but at home we so identified Christianity with "our way of life" that our own people are among the last in the world to be able to think globally. It comes as a surprise to the Christians of our Western world that it is now our mandate to *act* in accord with the universal brotherhood and unity we have been religiously championing all these centuries! It is just as surprising to Christians who hear this as it is to those who have long since ceased to claim any Christian affiliation.

It is no wonder that so few of those who seek global community today are led to think of Christianity as an asset in that search. One looks in vain for any reference to Christianity or Christian theologians or the "ecumenical spirit of Christianity" in the index of the study by Ward and Dubos. I fear that it is typical in this respect. When these scholars want to state what their hope is, they do so, not in religious terms, not even in terms of the highly acclaimed intellectual traditions of the West, but in biological terms:

Possibly it is precisely this shift of loyalty [to the global community] that a profound and deepening sense of our shared and inter-dependent biosphere can stir to life in us. That men can experience such transformations is not in doubt. From family to clan, from clan to nation, from nation to federation—such enlargements of allegiance have occurred without wiping out the earlier loves. Today, in human society, we can perhaps hope to survive in all our prized diversity provided we can achieve an ultimate loyalty to our single, beautiful and vulnerable Planet Earth.[44]

Although few of the most rigorous searchers for brotherhood turn to Christianity for any contribution (more turn to Marxism), the sensitive Christian can perceive in this search much that parallels the faith which knows "neither Jew nor Greek, . . . slave nor free, . . . male nor female." This is possible if he can get beyond the nationalistic and ideological captivities of that faith.

Let us admit that it is no easy matter to move from the Christian confession of the universal Lordship of Christ into the public arena of concern for global unity. A great many questions have to be ironed out. In particular, Christians have to rid themselves of a host of presuppositions, most of them imported into the faith from the long history of Christian imperialism. One such presupposition is the belief that the brotherhood that Christ offers has always to be acknowledged as his. We have not yet understood very much about the hidden work of the Christ, let alone about our responsibility to work with him incognito. We always want to elicit confessions of faith!

But if Jesus Christ is indeed Lord; if he is really at work in the world "to make and to keep human life human" (Paul Lehmann); if he is bringing men daily to participate in his gift of reconciliation, at many different levels of awareness and unawareness—then whenever prisoners are comforted, the naked clothed, and the hungry fed, Jesus Christ is himself intimately present. Can we who confess his presence not be prepared to find him among Marxists and humanists and others who strive for a more human world?

Whew!

Those who are working as Christians in the Third World today have grasped this connection better than we. It lies at the center of the so-called liberation theology. These words of the martyred priest Camilo Torres bear witness to it:

> I have no intention of proselytizing my Communist brothers, trying to get them to accept the dogma and to practice the cult of the Church. But this I am certainly working towards, that all men act according to their conscience, sincerely seek the truth, and love their neighbour in an effective way. The Communists must well know that I will not join their ranks, that I am not nor will I be a Communist, either as a Colombian, or as a sociologist, or as a Christian, or as a priest. However, I am ready to fight alongside them for common goals: opposing the oligarchy and the domination of the United States, in order to take power for the popular class.[45]

In the search for world brotherhood, authentic Christian faith may still shine here and there through the Babel confusion of sectarian loyalty and grasp the hands of others who acknowledge different flags.

The Search for a Soul

A third point at which it is possible to find a rich source of dialogue between the gospel and the human search for an alternative way is what we may call the search for a soul.

One of the great poet-prophets of our epoch, George Orwell, wrote the following lines in his journal in the year 1940:

> Reading Mr. Malcolm Muggeridge's brilliant and depressing book, *The Thirties*, I thought of a rather cruel trick I once played on a wasp. He was sucking jam on my plate, and I cut him in half. He paid no attention, merely went on with his meal, while a tiny stream of jam trickled out of his severed esophagus. Only when he tried to fly away did he grasp the dreadful thing that had happened to him. It is the same with modern man. The thing that has been cut away is his soul, and there was a period—twenty years, perhaps—during which he did not notice it.[46]

Since Orwell wrote these insightful lines, a great many more people in our tottering civilization have discovered that contemporary man is without a soul. This discovery is made, not only by thinkers and intellectuals but by many who know little of the tradition of the soul, either in its Greek or in its Judeo-Christian mode. A whole generation of young people, for example, almost on their own and for reasons that are genuinely mysterious, discovered the spiritlessness of their bourgeois homes and schools and went off to look for a world of color and sound. Often, to be sure, in sad and tragic ways; but nonetheless in ways so poignant and so beautiful that they could not be resisted even by the gray world of the dominant middle class. We are all a little more colorful today because of their rejection of the gray-flannel suits and the people who wore them.

But the search for soul is not merely a quest for color,

for the psychedelic. It is a quest for meaning: for a species of reason different from the "technical reason" (Tillich) that can in any case be better served by computers; for excellence beyond the mediocrity and plastic of the consumer society; for imagination that can transcend and judge the manipulations of the image-makers; for individuality against the encroachment of mass man. It is a quest for quality, a reaching out for transcendence.

Until recently an influential wing of Christian theology supposed that man's ability to envisage his being in transcendental terms had ended. He was depicted as virtually incapable of mystery; able to live out his days without raising the question of meaning. He was content to interpret his life strictly along existentialist lines, without recourse to the idea of essential being. In short he was secular man "come of age."

total immanence

No doubt there is still much truth in this picture. Perhaps the majority of men have been effectively stripped of that quality—imagination or whatever it is —which drives man to ask the question of being and makes him thirst for righteousness.

Yet it would be irresponsible today to overlook the fact that many who seemed content with the secular explanation in days of relative security have grown less satisfied with their vaunted maturity of late. There are many today who are ready to hope that "life is more than food and the body more than raiment." And some of those who needed bread and managed to get it have begun to know that "man does not live by bread alone."

Often the sense of loss of soul is experienced in strange quarters. In September 1969, John C. Bennett wrote in *Christianity and Crisis* the following report:

In his new book, *Religion, Revolution and the Future* . . .
Jürgen Moltmann has called attention to a remarkable development in the dialogue between Christians and Marxists in Europe. There Marxists have begun, he says, to ask
for "a new openness of men for transcendence." Meanwhile, Christians have been so intent on proving the immediate relevance of their faith to issues of social justice
that they have neglected the dimension of transcendence
in Christianity. Moltmann quotes Professor Prucha of
Prague: "Our Christian friends have awakened in us the
courage for transcendence. For a long time we Marxists
have tried to criticize and retard the Christian striving for
transcendence. Should it not, rather, be our task to encour-
age the Christians to be even more radical in their striving
for transcendence?"

. . . These comments are probably tentative and explora-
tory, but it is most significant that Marxists have detected
a missing dimension in the activist secular theologies that
are the current fashion.[47]

Dialectical materialism, as well as the garden-variety
materialism of the West's consumer society, here and
there is finally driven to ask whether matter alone can
explain the strange phenomenon called *Homo sapiens.* If
there is no transcendent quality against which our lives
can be measured, then neither can there be a goal, a
hope, a meaning by which they can be drawn. At the
outer edges of the secular society, where unabashed
secularity has been entered into with a will, men discover that their life begs the question of meaning. For
all its devotion to causes, as in the case of conscientious
Marxism, secular humanism finally must ask for a
deeper, more ultimate purpose by which that devotion
can be sustained. If such a purpose is not discovered,
even the most inspired secularism readily turns to cyni-

cism and nihilism—a thing that Solzhenitsyn has graphically documented for our age. George Grant has written, "Most men, when they face that there are no horizons in which their purposes are sustained, find that a darkness falls upon their wills."[48]

CONCLUSION

Many people both outside the Christian faith and within it have experienced the gospel as something real in our time. Many more might do so, were the conditions right. The gospel is no longer *necessarily* bound up with artificial religious forms, questions, and attitudes. It has become possible to see it as a reflection upon the real world and an attempt to meet the problems of the real world.

Out of a great variety of possibilities, I have singled out specific points of meeting in the foregoing discussion: places, that is, where Christian belief intersects with the struggles of men of goodwill; areas where the faith of the church coincides with the gropings of those who are trying to understand the human predicament and also to find a way into the future.

It has not been my assumption in any of this that these points of dialogue constitute a new revival of specifically religious interest. Nor do I see any immediate correlation between the world's questions and faith's answers—or its questions. As if one could move without difficulty from one to the other. The stumbling block remains. But many inessential barriers have been taken away. Especially from the world's side there is less possibility of pretense and bravado now. The real issues have become clearer.

For those Christians who have entered fully enough into the pain of the contemporary world, there is a certain excitement and anticipation inherent in our age. It is an age that has brought many thoughtful people to ask questions similar to those which Christian belief teaches one to ask; an age in which many who are "not of this fold" nevertheless long for answers to which Christians can relate the answers they have tried to hear.

But already in our discussion of this new openness to the reality of the gospel, we have had to encounter the other side of the coin. At every point where we have noticed the potentiality of dialogue with worldly ultimate concern, we have also had to draw attention to the fact that the all-too-typical Christianity of our culture seems to have little to say.

Thus, in connection with the analysis of the human predicament, so-called post-Christian men are even willing to pick up specifically Biblical concepts: sin, the demonic, the apocalyptic. But although individual theologians and others address these themes, the dominant Christianity of the churches seems to shy away from speaking in such drastic terms as these.

The case is similar when it comes to those points where the worldly search for alternatives seems to parallel certain aspects of Biblical faith. Under the impetus of humanitarian and planetary concern, scientists, economists, artists, and others seem ready to ask for ways into the future that are far more radical than anything dreamed of in our average congregations. To put it in a word, these worldly searchers for a way do not fear to dream and hope. They call for a whole new approach, a new style of life, a new heaven and a new earth! *It is almost as if they believed in the possibility of redemption!* Certainly they believe in the necessity of it.

Meanwhile, church Christianity, having refrained from drastic analysis of the problem, refrains equally from drastic remedies. It is as if we were still contemplating whether it would be fitting to move along to anything quite so different as . . . a religion of redemption! *(salvation)*

Nicodemus is ready to confess his sin. He is already asking for a way beyond it, a way into life. He comes by night. Will he find anyone in the night with whom to wrestle?

Chapter 2

The Unreality
of the Churches

INTRODUCTION

"WHAT TIME IS IT?"

I would like to begin with an extended parable:

On the island of Manhattan not far from Columbia University there stands a church building of impressive proportions. In its time, it was regarded as *the* church for uptown Manhattan members of its particular denomination. Even today it is physically capable of creating the impression of significance, perhaps of a certain Old World grandeur.

Its architectural style was borrowed from the period known as Romanesque. The sanctuary, with its rounded arches and striking mosaics, conveys an Eastern flavor. There are parlors, gymnasiums, auditoriums, schoolrooms, offices, a bowling alley, apartments for staff persons—well, it never seems to come to an end. The symbols of opulence are present everywhere, though in somewhat decadent and dated condition:

1. The pursuit of unreality
2. Our unreality about ourselves
3. Our unreality about the world
4. Our identification as/a social stratum

grand pianos, large and rich-looking sofas, a magnificent organ. In one parlor stands a modest round table on which a well-known American author wrote what is now a classic story—a symbol of the church's connections with the better traditions of our culture.

When I went to work in this church as a student I was quite charmed by all this. Who wouldn't be? Especially if one came, as I did, from a small village where the church consisted of a rather squatty white-brick building of Methodist character: one room, in fact, with a church shed behind it, used in those days only by youngsters playing hide-and-seek and other, less wholesome, games.

I was rather elated at the prospect of working there, too. It seemed that at last I was going to see something of the real relevance of the church in the modern world —the world of the concrete city, the slums, and racial unrest.

As part of my indoctrination, the minister took me for a long walk around the environs of the church. As we were strolling along, he pointed out how the area had deteriorated. That was obvious enough. Nearly all the people living there now, he told me, were blacks and Puerto Ricans—and therefore "Romans." Quite nominally, of course. He also intimated with some enthusiasm that just at that moment the city had begun to wreck the old apartment buildings and to put up new high rises. Naturally, he said, there would be some turnover in the population of the area as a result of this project. It was likely that new families would move in. Probably a reasonable percentage of them would be Protestant.

This last observation bothered me a little. If the

church was attempting to represent Christ in the concrete city, should it care so much whether people were
nominal Protestants or nominal Catholics? But I was
willing at that point to put this down to the minister's
Irish background. I knew that background well enough
from my own Orange Lodge relatives!

It wasn't long before I had discovered, however, how
seriously the distinction between nominal Protestantism and nominal Catholicism was taken. And a good
many other distinctions as well.

The church maintained a little chapel for black folk
several blocks away in the center of a predominantly
black district. I remember that a number of us, including the minister and his wife, went over there one night
around Thanksgiving time for a turkey dinner. The
black women didn't sit down with us, they served us.

Before long I had also noticed how often the laymen
and others spoke about the changes that would inevitably be brought about by the new building project. It
was evident that they entertained the same hopes that
the minister had expressed to me casually on our walk
—new Protestant families! New families of that particular brand of Protestantism, indeed!

Another constant subject of their conversation was
the past, the glorious past, when there had been five
hundred children in Sunday school, packed services,
and important people. I began to feel that this congregation lived only in the past—and in the future, when the
city's building project would give them back some of
their former glory.

In the meantime, everything went along as if nothing
had happened. On Sundays, though there might be
eighty-five people in the sanctuary that would seat

fifteen hundred, we marched in with full pomp and circumstance. The music was wonderful. Why shouldn't it have been? Every member of the choir was a professional musician. Quite a few were students at Juilliard, as I remember. And the organist was probably one of the best in the city. Paid, every one of them.

At the head of the processional, carrying one of the most ornate jeweled crosses I have ever seen, strode a tall young man. "Lucifer the Crucifer," my student colleague used to call him. He was studying ballet, and his style as we processed down the long aisle was exquisite. (Perhaps he was homosexual, but nobody spoke of that. And I wonder now whether any of us could have made any difference to his life if we had—if we had even befriended him. But then, he wasn't really a member of the congregation. Just one of its paid employees.)

The church had no need to worry about money. It was heavily endowed from the estates of "old families," no longer with us, alas. Besides, it owned a large cemetery in another part of the city. That was surprisingly lucrative, I gathered, though I could never imagine why. I suppose it had something to do with the fact that some wealthy people had their family plots there (among them, it was whispered, a prominent member of the Mafia). Anyway, the cemetery obviously figured large in the thinking of the parish. The great passion of the minister at that time, I discovered, was to construct a crematorium out there. Well—it wasn't macabre! Just good economics.

One evening the minister called together all those who taught in the little remnant of a Sunday school. Most of the teachers were middle-aged women, including the paid parish visitor, a dear little old soul who was genuinely without guile.

The minister had something important to say to all of us.

"This area," he announced, "is the most densely populated area in the entire world." He went into population statistics at some length: the overcrowded conditions, the lack of privacy, the squalor and poverty. I couldn't help remembering that he lived in a great mansion next door to the church.

Then, using a report that had been prepared for radio broadcast, he astonished all of us—especially the ladies —with the quantity and the enormity of the crime that was going on right around us: rape, drugs, robbery, murder, suicide, organized crime, prostitution—the works!

At the end of his long presentation he paused significantly, and then announced dramatically: "*This* is our parish."

At that moment, there was a knock on the door of the parlor in which we were meeting (we were sitting around the table of the famous author, I remember). Somebody had left the door a little ajar, and the visitor didn't wait for it to be opened, but pushed it back rather rudely. There she stood: a fat, homely little Puerto Rican girl, perhaps twelve or thirteen years of age.

"What time is it?" she demanded uncouthly, apparently unimpressed by our sedate little assembly.

The minister's face went hard with indignation. He looked around at all of us, obviously annoyed by this untimely interruption. Then he called out to the girl: "Can't you see we're having an important meeting here? Now run along . . . and don't bother us again!"

There was an embarrassed silence. The minister's

outburst had evidently surprised even the middle-aged ladies, though they were not unused to his sometimes imperious ways.

To put it all to rights again, the dear little parish visitor said quietly and with absolutely no malicious intent, just as an explanation, so to speak: "She's not one of ours, you know."

⚜ 1 ⚜

The Pursuit of Unreality

On Criticism of the Churches

None of us likes to engage publicly in criticism of the churches. We feel guilty about it when we do, especially those of us who remain within the churches. We feel we are being hypocrites. What right have we to be critical, to be biting the hand that feeds us? In our society, criticism is one of the worst vices. Critics are not popular persons. Nobody wants to be unpopular, especially clergy. And then, so often we find the wrong people agreeing with us when we criticize the churches. It's a little like criticizing your mother, and then finding your wife agreeing with every word you say. It's what she had been thinking all along!

In addition to all that, we are always conscious of the exceptions. There are congregations that really do know what time it is. Some ministers are giving their lives for justice and truth. Administrators are not always ecclesiastical bureaucrats attempting to secure their own jobs against the tide of irrelevancy and change. Not every church is like the one I described above. Indeed, in many respects the one I have just described is not at all typical.

The danger is that we become so conscious of all the exceptions, so afraid of being unfair, so imbued with what we assume must be Christian charity and humility, that we end by saying nothing. Or else we couch our criticism in such cautious language that it "dies the death of a thousand qualifications."

Listen carefully to clergy-talk in public. It's full of the most predictable, most defensive language, including language that defends *us* against the charge of negativism. The word "perhaps," for example. We can hardly say a sentence in public without putting that one in (often ungrammatically!): "Perhaps there is a need for greater concern about the young people." "We should perhaps ask whether the Methodists might not be offended if we took that course of action." "I wonder if it wouldn't be wise to perhaps check that out with the —well, perhaps the finance committee?"

A minimum of psychological sense will verify that such language almost certainly cloaks a heap of hostility. In fact, it is hardly possible to find a minister or active layperson today who, underneath it all, is not deeply critical of the churches. Get these people alone or in small congenial groups and only the most hardened positive thinkers can hold back the tide of abuse. The sense of the unreality of the churches is felt more strongly today by those who stay within the churches than by those who leave—or who never came in the first place. In the study of causes for leaving the parish ministry, to which I made reference earlier, the pastors were just as critical as the ex-pastors.[49]

For the most part, I think, the abuse of institutional

sociological method of church we're trying to follow

Christianity by institutional Christians is rather narrow, personal, even carping. It lacks the dimension of either sociological or theological depth that could take it out of the category of meanness. Ministers complain because they are so busy all the time with trivialities. Women complain because they have to bake pies and meet with other women. Most men feel that church services are designed for sopranos. Children are bored by Sunday school. So are their teachers.

All such criticism should be taken seriously, in a way. But what needs to be taken more seriously is that this criticism seldom rises above the level of abuse. It hardly ever becomes authentic "criticism": that is, faith's response to the *krisis* ("judgment") which "begins at the household of God." It remains abusive, petty. For the most part it is indulged in sub rosa, like children snipping at their teachers behind their backs. Only in this case it is never clear who the teachers are.

It seems to me entirely obvious why this is so. It is because we have not been able to permit authentic criticism to inform the public, everyday, theological, liturgical, and social life of our churches. When critique of any phenomenon is not permitted openly, we can be sure that it will be engaged in secretly. Besides, a new quality will be added just because it is not, and cannot, be open—the quality of resentment!

We resent having to play the game. We resent our own dishonesty. We resent having to bridle our tongues with perhapses. We resent having to save our honesty for "afterward": after church, after the board meeting, after presbytery, after class. We resent the unreality of the churches.

"It is very hard," said a well-known churchman, "to

stay within the church today and continue to be a real
person."

Why We Fear Criticism

When one asks *why* we have not been able to incorporate open criticism into the life of the churches, *why* we
play the game, *why* we save our honesty for "afterward," we have come to the mystery that I want to try
to unravel in this chapter.

My use of the word "mystery" is fully intentional, for
the matter is by no means easy to decipher. Nobody
compels us to refrain from criticism. There is no legisla-
tion about it. In some lands today there are elaborate
bureaucratic networks that ferret out all criticism and
negativism. Nobody would accuse the churches of that.
Yet of all the institutions in the world today there may
be none so efficient as the churches in squelching the
spirit of authentic criticism. It is not a matter of prohi-
bition so much as of a collective inhibition. Why? What
is at stake?

My thesis is this: Behind our collective refusal to
push negative analysis beyond a certain well-known
point, there lies an ideological commitment to the positive outlook of our culture. We have identified Christianity with that outlook. Today, when this cultural
optimism is no longer verified by experience, there is
even greater pressure upon the churches to preserve
that outlook intact.

In other words, we stop short of real criticism of the
churches because we are afraid of what such criticism,
if pursued far enough, would bring to the surface.
Great certainty, great commitment, does not fear criticism. But we are not confident that our ecclesiastical

loyalty—or even our faith—could stand exposure to the data that is present in contemporary experience. Like the Manhattan congregation of my parable, which lived in an idealized past and an imagined future, we perpetuate a certain image of the church and the world that no longer corresponds with reality. We are afraid that what reality there *is* might overwhelm us.

So there is an almost deliberate, almost conscious *pursuit* of unreality in Western Christianity. I think that it can only be explained by the presence of a deeply felt despair. Neither as a religion nor as a people can we cope with the questions that history has thrown up to us.

Three aspects of the unreality of the churches will be discussed in elaborating this thesis: (1) our unreality about ourselves, (2) our perpetuation of an unreal world view, and (3) our identification with a social stratum that is steeped in the same pursuit of unreality.

In all of this it is necessary to bear in mind the following points: First, we are here engaged in *self*-analysis. I am fully conscious of the fact that I am part of what I am trying to understand. Indeed, my own involvement in it is in a real sense the best entrée I can have into the problematic of it. Second, we are engaging in this criticism publicly, with the intention of raising it above the level of mere abuse of institutional Christianity and giving it theological depth. Third, we are not engaging in this critical task as an end in itself. Something else is to follow. It is a necessary step on the way to asking: What would be necessary for the churches to begin to be seen as real by people in our time? How could the churches come to participate in that same reality that not a few of our contemporaries are able to find in the Christian gospel?

The fundamental point is this: If we are still in the churches today, we have a responsibility before God, before our fellowmen, and before our own better traditions, to discover why the world finds the churches so unreal.

Jacques Ellul, in his book *Hope in Time of Abandonment,* has stated:

> It is not the unbelievers who are keeping God away. It is, on the one hand, a matter of structures. On the other hand, it is the responsibility of Christians and of the Church, who do not know how to be what God expects of them.[50]

We should bear this statement in mind as we begin to analyze the ecclesiastical pursuit of unreality.

2

OUR UNREALITY ABOUT OURSELVES

The Constantinian Assumption

In a controversial book in 1959, *How to Serve God in a Marxist Land,* Karl Barth cited with approval an East German pastor, General Superintendent Günther Jacob, of Cottbus, "who not long ago announced 'the end of the Constantinian era.' " Barth commented to his East German friends:

> Because I have a certain wariness about all theoretical formulations of a philosophy of history, I hesitate to make this expression my own. But it is certain that something resembling this approaching end begins to show itself dimly everywhere, but very sharply in your part of the world.[51]

Later I shall return to the East German aspect of this statement. At present I am concerned with how it applies to us in the West, especially in North America.

Many things about our real situation should lead us to the conclusion that we too live in the post-Constantinian era. Since 1959, when this term first began to appear among us, it has become ever more evident that no Christian churches in the Western world can legitimately draw upon the Constantinian assumption. Yet we all, in one degree or another, continue to live on the basis of that assumption.

The truth is, it *ought* not to have been possible for us to accept the Constantinian assumption for at least the past century. Sir Kenneth Clark would say for the last two centuries at least![52]

It is not as if we had no warnings about this from inside the church itself. More than a century ago, that troublesome Dane, Søren Kierkegaard, was announcing the death of Christendom. Quoting John 5:44—"How can ye believe, which receive honor one of another?"—he wrote:

> This again is the death-sentence to all official Christianity. This prodigious castle in the air: Christian states, kingdoms, lands; this playing with millions of Christians who reciprocally recognize one another in their mediocrity, yet are all of them believers—this whole thing rests upon a foundation which, according to Christ's own words, makes it impossible to believe.
>
> The Christianity of the New Testament is to love God in opposition to men, to *suffer* at the hands of men for one's faith. . . . Only that is to believe; to receive honour from men makes it impossible to believe.[53]

There is much in Kierkegaard's *Attack Upon Christendom* that is still exceptionally timely. His word here, for example, about the insipid quality of ecclesiastical life: people reciprocally recognizing one another in their mediocrity! Echoing it, Ellul has written of the contemporary churches:

> The Church was called to be made up of the weak, the poor, and the lowly, and to have little power and glory. We know what happened to that. Yet it is not so much the fact that she is composed of the bourgeoisie and "the rich." ... What seems to me important is the mediocrity, for she is just as mediocre where her membership is proletarian and antibourgeois. It is not the weakness or the small numbers, the decrease in active membership, or the fact that she draws from a certain social stratum which troubles me. It is the mediocrity.[54]

Although in this and in many other respects Kierkegaard's analysis is uncanny in its foresight, it is also a dated work. For since this Danish Socrates took his daily constitutional in the square outside his rich father's house, talking to the common people and the students and being observed by his enemies, the churches have grown visibly smaller and less impressive. In his time, they were still full and apparently powerful. This is one reason why we didn't hear about Kierkegaard until long after his time. It's different now.

Let me make the difference somewhat graphic. About two years ago, I went to divine service in the Vor Frue Kirke—the cathedral of Copenhagen—where Kierkegaard had sat and fumed inwardly at the sermons of Bishop Mynster and looked fearfully in the direction of his beloved Regina. It is one of those great European edifices, famous for the statues of Thorvaldsen. The royal box is still there and is sometimes occupied.

Since I couldn't understand Danish anyway, I occupied my time with a little statistical research during the sermon. There were approximately one hundred persons in the church, not counting the choirboys, who were three galleries above us physically and heaven knows how far mentally. I didn't count the great Thorvaldsen figures of the disciples either, from whom I noticed one was conspicuously absent: Judas. "He usually stands *there*," said the vicar afterward, pointing to the pulpit.

Of the hundred persons present in this enormous room, I reckoned approximately 65 to be over seventy years of age; 20 to be between fifty and seventy; and 10 to be somewhere between twenty and fifty. I was among the younger ones present. The remaining five or so were small children, carried, no doubt, whither in a few years they would not go!

It was heartwarming, though, to notice that the greatest number of persons were gathered around the pulpit, which in this church was halfway down the aisle, right across from the royal box in the first gallery and almost on a level with royalty. How fine! I thought. These faithful Lutheran souls still come to hear the Word of God, at least. Then I noticed that all the hearing aids were in that section.

But the point is this: Everything went along just as always, as if nothing had happened. The liturgy, I suppose, was almost the same as it had been in Søren Kierkegaard's time. Stirring triumphal hymns; the ministers in full gown with those fanciful ruffled Scandinavian collars; the people well but modestly

dressed; an atmosphere of "business as usual." Everything just as it had been in New York when we strode
down the aisle behind our jeweled cross. I had the distinct impression that nobody else in the church that
morning had any reflective awareness of all that emptiness.

Power Through Proximity to Power

Heart of issue

(most important section)

In North America we congratulate ourselves that our
churches have not become so empty as that. On the
whole that is true. The death of Christendom is more
visible in Western Europe than it is here. So far. And
that, as I shall try to show presently, seems to me due
to the peculiar character of our form of Christian establishment.

The external visibility of Christendom's demise is
not the only test of the fact. Even where visibility is
concerned, there can be only relative distinctions.
European churches are emptier than ours. The primary
factor in the Christendom assumption, however, was
never so much the question of numerical strength as it
was the question of proximity to power. Numerical
strength became important only when power moved
from an oligarchy to a class. No doubt that is why the
question "How many?" has been so important for us in
North America. We should not be led astray by this
concentration on numbers. The concern beneath it is a
concern for power.

This fundamental presupposition of Christendom
Christianity—namely, the search for power through
proximity to power—has been beautifully documented
in Yves Congar's *Power and Poverty in the Church*. Toward the end of the book, Congar pleads:

The Holy Roman Empire no longer exists, but there still remain in the Church many titles and insignia, many elements of ceremonial and so forth of her visible aspect, borrowed at some time from the dazzling imperial splendor. Surely it is high time, and surely it would be to everyone's advantage, "to shake off the dust of Empire that has gathered since Constantine's day on the throne of St. Peter." These words were spoken by John XXIII.[55]

This is well said. All the same, it may not necessarily be a gesture of humility when the church divests itself of the "vestiges of Empire." Nor is it necessarily an indication of the desire to seek an alternative to the way of Christendom. It may rather be "to everyone's advantage," including the church's. For power does not lie with kings and empires now. The tokens of courtly life and of the old aristocracy no longer benefit the church. It may be only a new bid for proximity to power when churches move to divest themselves of old symbols.

In fact, if Protestantism in North America has been quantitatively successful for longer than Catholicism in Latin Europe, it is partly because Protestantism soon found out the direction in which power had shifted. It went from the palaces of kings to the houses of merchants and highly placed bureaucrats. And for a long time it stayed there.

But the crisis of Christendom Christianity today is that the precise location of power is unknown. Who can latch on to it? It is altogether elusive, like the authorities in Kafka's *The Castle*. We will return to this observation later.

locus of power unknown!

In terms of the quest for power through proximity to power, we North American Christians show ourselves to be just as tied, intellectually and emotionally, to the

Christendom mentality as our European counterparts. We remember our powerful past. We hope for more power in the future. We openly court power. We lay our plans around the concepts of power and influence. We judge our "success" in terms of power.

Sometimes this is so blatant in us that only the dullest observers could miss it. Recently in connection with an educational experiment in our city, an influential layman proposed that a program of Christian education be included in the curriculum of the experimental school. The constitution of the school stated unequivocally that the school was nondenominational in character. The layman in question could scarcely comprehend it when some of the "free thinkers," as he styled them, objected —as they did, strenuously! In defense of his stand, he insisted that surely on this continent there could be only a tiny minority of such free thinkers as these.

Most Christians are not so naïve in their quest for power, but the quest is scarcely ever absent from our calculations. Ministers and church courts expect to be heard because they are ministers and church courts. Observe what happens if the press doesn't show up for a church conference if you don't think so. Christian educators and concerned laymen expect to establish schools of theology in secular universities without serious opposition. Laymen in some congregations still speak as though it were socially prestigious to go to church. In the head offices of churches, questionnaires and surveys are devised that betray no awareness whatsoever of the demise of the whole grand scheme of Christendom. On the contrary they assume that ministers and congregations will assess themselves in strictly quantitative terms. "Stop speaking out of both sides of your mouth," wrote one pastor to his church administration. "You urge prophetic, creative ministry, yet judge us by old statistical values. You have us in a trap."[56]

It is understandable that our bondage to the Constantinian assumption is deep. After all, it was sixteen centuries in the making. Even when we have discarded intellectual aspects of it, we are committed to it at emotional depths that are almost automatic. For instance, no one ever asks me, "What is the level of theological involvement and excitement at your seminary?" I am only asked, "How many students do you have?" Or some who know a little more about the struggle today try to find out what sort of influence our institution has on the university of which it is a part. Even *I* ask these things!—and feel embarrassed that there are so few students of theology and that we have so little tangible influence. This feeling persists even though some of the students are probably more authentic persons than were many of my generation in the seminary—during the days when seminaries could still attract the affable young men. And even though some of the involvement that we have in the university may be more genuine, more closely related to the real concerns of the university, than used to be the case when clergymen were presidents of universities.

or community where it's located

Our Uneasiness
with an Alternative Image of the Church

Our commitment to the Christendom image of the church is nowhere more obvious than when we are confronted by a genuine alternative to it.

Karl Rahner, today the greatest theologian of the Roman Catholic Church, which traditionally is perhaps the most triumphalistic of all the churches, has written:

> My thesis is this: Insofar as our outlook is really based on today, and looking towards tomorrow, the present situation of Christians can be characterized as that of a *diaspora*. . . .[57]

The word "diaspora" means a scattering, a dispersion. It was used to refer to the dispersion of the Jews throughout the Roman Empire at the time of the apostles. It would be appropriate always to hear this word against the background of the Tower of Babel myth. The builders of Babel say to one another: "Come, let us build ourselves a city, and a tower with its top in the heavens, and let us make a name for ourselves, *lest we be scattered abroad upon the face of the earth.*" (Gen. 11:4, italics added.) It is just the prospect of a scattering, a diaspora, that drives anxious men to grasp after power through proximity to power. The church, which according to Scripture is created by the power of the descending Spirit of God at Pentecost (Acts, ch. 2), has always been tempted by the Babel quest for power. The fear of dispersion is great in fallen humanity. But Rahner says that the situation of Christians in the world today is already one of diaspora. He continues:

> The Christendom of the Middle Ages and after, peasant and individualistic petty-bourgeois Christendom, is going to disappear with ever-increasing speed. For the causes which have brought about this process in the West are still at work and have not yet had their full effect.[58]

We are moving, Rahner claims, toward a future in which the Christendom mentality will be obviously and totally out of place.

Diaspora!
see p. 178

At that future date there will be Christian communities all over the world, though not evenly distributed. Everywhere they will be a *little* flock, because mankind grows more quickly than Christendom and because men will not be Christians by custom and tradition, through institutions and history, but . . . they will be Christians only because of their own act of faith attained in a difficult struggle and perpetually achieved anew.[59]

Rahner conjures up a picture of the Christian life in such a setting that is quite unlike anything the majority of Christians have experienced during these twenty centuries. The Christian of that post-Constantinian situation is never secure:

His faith is constantly threatened from without. Christianity receives no support, or very little, from institutional morality, custom, civil law, tradition, public opinion, normal conformism, etc. Each individual has to achieve it afresh for himself; it is no longer simply "a heritage from our fathers." Each individual must be won to it afresh, and such a recruitment can appeal only to personal decision, to what is independent and individual in a man, not to that in him which makes him a homogeneous part of the masses, a product of his situation, of "public opinion" and of his background. Christianity ceases to be a religion of growth and becomes a religion of choice.[60]

We can scarcely envisage such a picture of the church. It eludes our imagination, even though it is evidently closer to the New Testament picture of the koinonia than anything we have had in the sixteen centuries of Constantinian Christendom. We have been conditioned to read even the New Testament from this side of the Edict of Milan. We read it as the meager beginnings of something that later on "made it." And even if the idea of "little flocks here and there" is not beyond our intellectual grasp, it is beyond our emotional and organizational grasp. We are committed to the Constantinian approach at depths that are truly abysmal. To the quest for power through proximity to power.

The plain fact is that we do not have power and, in these days, can no longer reasonably expect to achieve real proximity to it. Indeed, we cut a ridiculous figure in the world when we behave as if we had this power. In Europe the church conjures up the image of a proud, sad old lady, strutting about in a supermarket, dressed in the clothes of a bygone era, and calling peremptorily for the clerks to come and attend to her order. Here in North America the image has a more swinging character.[61] But it is fundamentally the same, and the effect is just as unconvincing. We are trying to drag into the twenty-first century an image of the church that has not been real since the eighteenth century or earlier.

The pity of it is that precisely by pursuing this sort of power we cut ourselves off from the power that *is* present in our situation. It is a different kind of power, to be sure. It cannot be used for personal gain. But it is, all the same, power, and it belongs to the very essence of Christ's church. The trouble is that from the vantage point of Constantinian power, it is bound to look like weakness, or to be overlooked altogether. We are not ready to relinquish that vantage point. Like the church in my introductory parable, we are so busy remembering the past and awaiting a future that repeats the past that we neglect the real opportunities of the present—

[margin handwriting: Cut ourselves off from power that counts!]

even when they come knocking at our door.

Is that because we sense the costliness of availing ourselves of the power that rightly belongs to Christ's church? In order to realize that power, we would have to abandon once and for all the power quest at the heart of the Constantinian assumption. For the power that Christ offers his church is available only to those who are willing to become weak and afraid and little: weak with the weak, afraid with the fearful, little with the insignificant. Humiliated!—as the whole race of man is being humiliated and brought low today. It is the power of those who go into the night of contemporary man; who give up all that insulates them against that night, all the comforting accumulations of the centuries; who are ready to be there, in the night, for Nicodemus with his anxious questions.

⚜ 3 ⚜

OUR UNREALITY ABOUT THE WORLD

Bound to a World View

Our unreality about ourselves is not the most serious aspect of this problem. At a still more insidious level, the sense of unreality that pervades the churches today can be traced to the image of the world we carry about with us as Christians. What the churches inevitably attempt to drag into the future is not merely an earlier, grander image of themselves, but an entire world view. It is the particular world view, whatever it is, that was associated with the grander image of themselves. What the Manhattan congregation dreamed of was not just a return of the good old days with five hundred children in the church school and a full house on Sunday mornings. They envisaged the whole neighborhood transformed—filled again with wealthy and influential Protestant families. They had to indulge in the greater sociological dream, for the ecclesiastical dream depended on it.

There are many variations in the world views we cling to. In West Germany the world view that Protestants evidently wish to perpetuate—because it somehow marks the height of their power—is heavily informed by the culture of the sixteenth and seventeenth centuries. You have only to study their hymnbooks casually to realize that. There is hardly anything from the twentieth century; nothing at all from the nineteenth (hymns of that period have been expurgated, partly on account of the Nazi misuse of nineteenth-century sentiments); a few from the eighteenth. The great majority of the hymns come from the triumphant age of Protestantism in Germany.

On the same basis, it would have to be said that the world view we North American churchmen attempt to carry into the twenty-first century is deeply influenced by the nineteenth century. This is still true, I think, notwithstanding the spate of twentieth-century hymns encountered in the new hymnbooks of the various denominations. Nineteenth-century sentiments and musical conventions still prevail in most of them.[62]

Our clinging to an unreal, outdated view of the world is not merely a harmless preoccupation—a matter of simply clinging to favorite old hymns. The hymns are indicative of our state of mind. But since there are many complex reasons for attachment to church music and the like, I shall quickly turn to a different kind of evidence for the claim that we are bound to an outdated world view.

The Perpetuation of a Myth

It should be acknowledged that we have made a considerable show of interest in finding out what the contemporary world is all about. That is why, in my introductory story, I was careful to include the information that the minister took me on a walk around the environs of the church as part of my indoctrination; also that we met as a teaching staff to discuss the character of "our parish."

On the national and international Christian scenes, the churches have spent great sums of money staging conferences, special studies, and programs of concern that embody this same goal. People are flown about the world on study tours. Oceans of mimeographed and printed data circulate around the globe from the head offices of churches and councils of churches. Surely no Christians have ever been more inundated with informative and resource material than we are! Moreover, we are all thoroughly initiated into the need for relevance, action, caring, world development, and whatnot.

But in the first place, the great bulk of all this material, all these plans, remains at the paper stage; in the second place, the whole enterprise serves to perpetuate a very questionable myth.

Albert van den Heuvel illustrates the first contention. As one who has spent a good deal of his life in committees and head offices, he knows the problem from the inside. In his *The Humiliation of the Church*, van den Heuvel writes:

> It is a scandal to see the beautiful ecumenical documents which the churches drew up together far away from the place where God had set them and which were never applied at home. If somebody has sufficient courage to make a study of cynicism, he should buy the reports of all major ecumenical gatherings, read them, and see what the churches said together. Then he should go to the balcony of his house and look over his city at the churches that are standing there, from which steeples have risen to heaven since the Middle Ages, and see how nothing has happened to them.[63]

Besides being more impressive in the talking than in the doing, all this bustle of study and concern about the contemporary world keeps alive in the ecclesiastical mind the convenient myth that we can do it if only we will. It perpetuates a view of the world that is at least as old as the white man's civilization in North America and was particularly strong during the nineteenth century. It is the innocent belief that the world is somehow waiting for our enlightened and problem-solving Christian presence. "This is our parish."

Let me state that again, only this time in terms of what such a world view protects us from encountering. Keeping alive the vision of ourselves as doers, liberators, and problem solvers, keeps us from catching on to the truth that many angry people are trying to communicate to us affluent North Americans today—namely, that we are part of the problem! That precisely our doing, our saving and liberating, our disseminating and developing, our preaching and ordering and sharing and teaching and exemplifying, and so on, are very close to the root cause of the world's malaise.

We want a world in which problems are soluble—chiefly by technological means. We want to believe *ourselves* to be the bearers of the solution, of salvation! Karl Jaspers was right, in my opinion, when he wrote: "Our thinking is not wholly serious until we come to the end of our know-how. Our age must learn that some things are beyond 'doing.' "[64]

At the ethical level we perpetuate a world view in which everything can still be done—and by us! At the theological level we sustain the same world view by addressing ourselves to questions to which answers can be given. The trouble is that they are mostly questions nobody asks. Well, there are people who ask them. There are always people who ask whether it is still possible to believe in God, or whether modern man can accept the idea of miracles, or whether the Bible is the Word of God, or what Christianity teaches about marriage and the family. These are all important questions, in their way. But we mistake them for the basic questions—which are only rarely the questions that people ask. They are the questions that people live with and are.

It is significant that at least two of the most recent and loudly trumpeted movements in theology, in their reception by North Americans, betrayed a high degree of this ecclesiastical propensity to skirt the real question. I am referring to the theology of the "death of God" and the theology of hope. I suspect the same judgment can be made about the current interest in a theology of liberation.

Everybody became excited about the "death of God"

fiasco. In its profoundest representatives, Dorothee Sölle in Germany and Thomas Altizer in the United States, this theology was not a shallow thing. Nor was it untimely. But in terms of its popular front and its reception by the churches, it was clearly a diversion from the real problem.

The real problem is not the "death of God" but, as I have assumed from the outset of this study, the death of man. The latter is closer to what Nietzsche meant when he first invented the phrase "death of God." We would be coming closer to it still if we translated it "death of meaning." The real question that haunts our Nicodemus is not whether God exists, but whether it is any longer meaningful to use the term "Man"—capital *M*.

Novelists, playwrights, and artists have known that for decades. "What are human beings *for?*" asks the wise fool Vonnegut.[65] But neither as a people nor as churchmen in North America are we prepared for such a question. So we keep it remote. We talk about God, and cry that he is dead, or that he is certainly alive!

Again, many churchmen approved heartily of Moltmann's *Theology of Hope*. We could not wait to have representatives from Europe and South America to give us the latest word on hope. Not many people actually made it all the way through Moltmann's difficult book—a few found Rubem Alves easier going. On the whole, the slogan itself was sufficient for our theological and homiletical fires. It confirmed for a great many people who had grown anxious about our "national philosophy of optimism" (Sidney Hooke) that we Christians could still support it wholeheartedly.

What we should have been doing, instead, was to take seriously the real pessimism and despair that is just beneath the surface of our society. Lacking a frame of reference for exposure to that darkness, the majority chose to interpret the theologians of hope in a predictable way as optimists speaking out against contemporary pessimism. Few find Moltmann's current work, *The Crucified God*, so much to their liking.

Where to Turn?

It isn't only that we *want* to keep the nineteenth-century world view going, with its optimistic estimate of man, its technological redemptionism, its religion of progress. I think we don't know anything else.

At various levels of consciousness, to be sure, we are aware that this world view has been called into question by the series of events called "the twentieth century," beginning August 1, 1914. Some of us are deeply and anxiously aware of that. But we don't know what to put in its place. As Michael Novak has written:

> Politicians protecting the "free" world, industrialists building a better world through chemistry, scientists seeing themselves as the vanguard of evolution, professors educating young persons for a better tomorrow—all have reason to resist the notion that progress is a self-deception masking self-destruction. . . . The myth of progress through the technical solution of problems does not adequately express the human situation. It is shallow, one-dimensional, repressing, and destructive. But when one loses faith in it, where can one turn?[66]

Sidney Pollard, in his study *The Idea of Progress*, anticipates Novak's question with the answer, "Today, the only possible alternative to the belief in progress would be total despair."[67]

It is particularly hard for us North Americans, because our society is the special product of the religion of progress. As George Grant has said, we have no history before the age of progress.[68] It might be expected that Christianity, which certainly does have a history before the age of progress, could have provided some sort of alternative between progress and despair. But our kind of Christianity has been so heavily informed by the positive outlook of modernity that we Christians are no less appalled at the prospect of the end of progress than our nonchurched neighbors.

The truth is that few Christians get so far as to reflect seriously on the experience of negation, which has been the characteristic experience of men in this century. Those who do seem able to face the negative only by administering strong doses of otherworldly positivism as an antidote to despair. "Earth has no sorrows that heaven cannot heal."

The majority of us, however, being liberal and thoroughly this-worldly, prefer to grit our teeth and remain positive, optimistic, hopeful. Afraid of falling into anxiety, and lacking the courage to enter our own night, we keep up as best we can the semblance of light bequeathed to us by our fathers. "Better to light one candle than to curse the darkness," we say to one another. So we stop short of the drastic probing that has led many of our secular contemporaries to speak again about sin and the demonic and the end. That's just cursing the darkness, we tell ourselves. On the contrary, in the name of all that is true and lovely and of good report, we stand on the edge of night and cry that it is growing lighter.[69]

In the meantime, Nicodemus is waiting in the dark.

❧ 4 ❧

OUR IDENTIFICATION
WITH A SOCIAL STRATUM

Establishment

Not only do we have an unreal vision of ourselves
and of the world in which we find ourselves today. We
are also almost inextricably bound up with a social stratum whose whole raison d'être seems to be the preserva-
tion of a way of life that is unreal, and dangerously so.

What to call that social stratum is a problem. It is not
very useful in our context to name it "The Middle
Class," or "The Bourgeoisie." These categories have
been spoiled by Marxist usage, which is too narrowly
economic for the North American situation. The social
stratum in question cuts across income brackets and
social status. The term "Middle America" might come
closer to it; but that too poses problems—for Canadians,
for example.

Perhaps the better term is one that has been used by
sociologists such as Slater and Roszak: "the dominant
culture." It is best described in two ways: (*a*) *via
negativa,* by what it excludes, namely, the very poor, the
protest groups, the native peoples, most of the French,
the blacks, critical intellectuals, the various forms of the
counter culture, other smaller minorities; (*b*) *via
positiva,* by what it stands for, namely, a positive outlook that contains such concepts as progress, technological optimism, the belief in North American goodness
and innocence, the conviction that there are no insolu-
ble problems.

The interests of this social stratum are closely bound

up with our cultural Christianity. In fact, if the churches have been able to keep going for so long as if nothing had happened, it is only because there has been a certain demand for that kind of unreality. The law of supply and demand applies here. A social stratum exists whose interests are served by this genius for "business as usual" displayed by the churches. Without the demand for this product, how would it have been possible for Christianity to carry on in the style of "Christendom" for so many decades beyond its demise as a dominant intellectual and cultural force? Without this need, how would it have been possible for tens of thousands of churches on this continent to keep going, economically and institutionally? Without the money bequeathed to it by the "old families"; without the continued attendance of remnants of those families (who came in all the way from Long Island); without the tax exemptions granted to it by the voters; without the determination of the well-to-do (including also criminal elements!) to maintain their prestige even in death— without all that, something about the Manhattan church of my parable would have had to change long before now! It has not had to change; it has been able to continue as if nothing had happened, for the simple reason that it serves the needs and the interests of a particular social entity. And so has the Vor Frue Kirke of Copenhagen; and so have innumerable other such religious institutions, great and small, throughout the Western world.

What I am saying, to put it in other words, is that we have been dependent upon a certain arrangement known as "Establishment."

Now it is immediately necessary to clear up a serious

misunderstanding about this concept. North American churchmen are prone to believe that the term "Establishment" does not apply in our situation. The informed within my own denomination, for example, will point with pride to the pioneering struggle of Egerton Ryerson, who kept at least one denomination from establishing itself in our part of the New World. We congratulate ourselves heartily when we hear of the European establishments, with their bondage to the State (which "pays the piper"), their perfunctory ceremonies of Confirmation (a West German pastor friend of mine calls them "Passing Out" ceremonies), and their shocking discrepancy between statistical and actual church membership.

But these legal (*de jure*) establishments and our vaunted freedom from them have only served to blind us to the deeper meaning of the concept of Establishment. In many ways the legal establishments of old Europe are less effective, less insidious, than our North American form of establishment. For one thing, when something is out in the open, named and labeled, it tends to be less potent. For another thing, the European form of establishment is largely a matter of *form*. With us, on the contrary, the establishment thrives at the level of *content*.

What I mean, concretely, is this: In North America the establishment of Christianity consists of the identification of the Christian faith with the values, goals, and ways of the dominant culture. It is not something that exists at the legal level—though there are certainly important vestiges of that in our situation too. It exists rather as a de facto cultural alliance. It functions at the level of what is meant by the term "way of life," or if you like, at the level of an ideology.

In other words, the establishment that is characteristic of Christian experience on this continent expresses itself primarily, not in a system of church tax, government recognition, and such externals, but in the cultural assumption that we are a Christian people. Any attack on our way of life is automatically an attack on Christianity. Hence for many in this social stratum, the struggle against Communism has taken on the proportions of a holy war.

The Making of an Establishment

How such an establishment came to be, historically, is a complex story and cannot be told adequately in this context. But the bare outlines of it are not difficult to trace.

The beginnings of the New World coincided with a new vision of man's place in the universe. Out of the apocalyptic darkness of fourteenth-century Europe, during which a third of the population was carried off by the plague, a new image of man emerged. The struggle of this new *imago hominis* to realize its possibilities lies behind all the significant revolutions of the period we call modern.

The new image was first expressed in the works of the great scholars of the Renaissance. Gradually it manifested itself in the common life. Man began to rid himself of the propensity to fatalism—a fatalism that accepted his domination by nature, disease, poverty, and human institutions as being God-given. He began to think of himself as free, autonomous. He dreamed of mastering his environment, of becoming the "heroic steersman"[70] of the ship of history. It was a highly positive vision of man and his world. Never before had men dared to think so confidently about human possibilities.

The New World was at once the product of this vision and one of its primary inspirations. "America" became the place where, in the most satisfying sense, all this was going to happen.

Men tried to make it happen in Europe, too. They are still trying. But there were barriers in Europe that European man did not encounter in the great, free expanses of "America." The structures of the Old World order, with its remnants of feudalism, its poverty, its crippling wars, and its pervasive, pagan pessimism, could not be easily conformed to the new vision. The attempt to make them conform was a heroic one, reaching a certain climax in the French Revolution. An entire new social class had arisen in response to the new image of man—the so-called bourgeoisie. It became the destiny of this class to throw off the old structures, along with the fantasies that had fostered them, so far as possible.

Christianity was deeply implicated in those old structures. Indeed, the primary ideological matrix of those structures and institutions was a version of the Christian religion. The attack of the champions of the new vision upon the established powers therefore had to be an attack upon the church. It was inevitable that in the fall of kings and nobles, a religion that had given itself to kings and nobles would also be confronted by the avenger.

But the revolution inspired by the new image of man never really succeeded in Europe. It is a mark of its failure that the most recent heirs of the new vision, the

Marxists, can be heard even today using the same rhetoric about their various experiments as the eighteenth-century humanists used of "America."

In the New World, on the other hand, it was possible almost from the outset for the newly emergent image of man to inform the patterns and structures of society. From the beginning, the social stratum that was dominant on this continent was that class which had most fully grasped the implications of the new vision of man's possibilities.

Christianity in this New World, strictly following the ingrained dictates of the Constantinian assumption, moved toward this new seat of power.

I am not implying that it was all carefully planned. There were innumerable "accidental" reasons why Christianity became such a middle-class phenomenon on this continent. It is not necessary, however, to eliminate from our account a certain amount of Constantinian cunning on the part of the architects of our kind of Establishment. If they declined legal Establishment on the European patterns, it was not purely out of Christian altruism; nor was it merely because there were so many nonconformists among them. One suspects that the struggle against legal Establishment was informed by a highly astute worldly wisdom, which recognized that a church such as the Church of England, with its roots in monarchy and aristocracy, would not be able to wield power in the New World. The world had moved into another phase—the phase of the developer, the planner, the producer, the financier. And now it would be important for the church, if it were to influence the destiny of this people, to make friends with the new man.

The extent to which such calculations can be attributed to our Christian forebears on this continent is of course limited. It would certainly be farfetched to impute to them pure rationality and foresight. Like all human institutions, and like the human species itself, Christendom has a strong penchant for survival. This will to survive can often detect intuitively the direction in which it should move. Certainly it is not merely an accident of history that the really *established* churches in the New World have not been those, like the Anglican, that were bound to the older image of man, but those which were able to appeal to the social stratum that had captured the spirit of the new vision.

"Accentuate the Positive"

There is, however, a special twist in this New World installment of the establishment of Christianity.

The Constantinian assumption—the ecclesiastical pursuit of power through proximity to power—is not difficult to apply, at least in theory, when power is located in an emperor, an oligarchy, or some similar limited and getatable entity. But how achieve proximity to a class, a whole social stratum?

The only way that this can happen is if the church adapts itself, including its worship, its theology, its morality, its organizational structures, to the ways and purposes of that social stratum. It may maintain a certain distance from that stratum (so, in its way, did the old church of the Holy Roman Empire) by standing for a *higher* morality, a more *expansive* vision of truth. But it must not fundamentally contradict the outlook of that cultural stratum. It may even go far toward a prophetic critique of the *status quo*, as did the social gospel movement. But it will <u>only</u> enjoy proximity to that power if it <u>continues to give evidence of a basic accep-tance of the way of life adopted by the social stratum in question.</u>

There is a still more complex twist to this New World version of Christian establishment. Fundamental adherence to the outlook of the dominant culture in North America has meant one thing in particular, namely, the <u>maintenance of a consistently *positive* approach toward existence.</u> "Accentuate the positive, eliminate the negative, and don't mess with Mister In-between!" The <u>official vision is an optimistic</u> one. What cannot be permitted is any *serious* questioning of the basic tenets of this optimism, particularly in the idea of progress. As Reinhold Niebuhr wrote:

Official vision

> The prestige of the idea of salvation through history has been so great that the portion of the Christian church in most intimate contact with modern culture practically capitulated to the modern scheme of salvation, seeking to save the relevance of Christianity by making it appear to be an anticipation of the modern idea of progress.[71]

Where the positive alone is acceptable, the negative can be entertained only to the extent that it can serve the positive. North American Christianity has not al-together ignored life's negations. From one point of view, it has been preoccupied with them. But it has not allowed itself to entertain an unresolved negative. Sick-ness, doubt, anxiety, uncertainty, insecurity, meaning-lessness, death—all of these could be tackled by the typical Christianity of our experience. But only if—in point three of the sermon!—they were overcome, re-solved.

The extent of our exploration of life's *questions* has depended on our ability to *answer* them convincingly. So our excursions into the night, in the typical Christianity of this continent, have not been very extensive. If our Christianity has a reputation for being rather shallow (which, among Christians of other parts of the world, it has), that is largely the reason. Having been bound to provide solutions for every problem we looked at, we have not looked very far into the problems.

Shallow Christianity

Consequently it is not surprising that the churches in our society have not been able to speak of contemporary human experience in terms of sin, the power of the demonic, or a destructive omega. Such terms as these, radically interpreted, are fundamentally inconsistent with the world view of the social stratum with which the churches are aligned. The worldly wise—Menninger, Vonnegut, and the others—have been free to go far into the contemporary experience of negation. If official Christianity stops short on the edge of the night and cries that it is growing lighter, it speaks not out of faithfulness to the gospel. Rather, it is keeping faith with the ideology of that social stratum with which we have made our cultural covenant. It is a matter of maintaining our establishment.

It is precisely this that is being referred to today in the Third World and elsewhere as: "the ideological misuse of the Christian faith."

The Ultimate Irony

The ultimate irony of our condition as churches, however, is that although we are still acting on the Constantinian assumption, the power no longer resides where we assume it does. We are courting a social stratum that here and there still "needs" us, but it has nothing to give by way of power. It is itself victimized by power.

I am not proposing that the dominant culture of this continent is impotent, only that it is no longer really in charge, as the adjective "dominant" would suggest. I am assuming that it is still capable of exercising great influence in the world, much of it bad, so far as the majority of the world's peoples are concerned. This determination to hang on to the positive outlook; this insistence that our way of life represents the highest pinnacle of human achievement; this vision of the world as a place where everything can still be done, and by us, a world in which there are no limits—such an outlook is obviously still capable of doing a great deal of damage on earth. Especially when it is combined with an absolute refusal to reflect on the charge that we are, in fact, an oppressing, warmongering, overconsuming, and wasteful people.

Although the analysis of power should not overlook the dominant culture of this continent, the assumption that the power is located in us, that we are really in charge, is finally too naïve. We ought not to let Marxists and others lead us astray on this point. The real power is not in the hands of the bourgeoisie. The Middle Americans, like all the rest, are in its hands. So to act after the manner of doctrinaire Marxism and make the middle class the special enemy is to turn the whole struggle of contemporary man into a sort of nineteenth-century melodrama. By the same token, the Christian propensity to court the dominant culture on the assumption that that is where the power lies is equally naïve and pathetic.

It is pathetic, above all, because it assumes that there is no alternative for the church but to continue along the lines of the Constantinian assumption. I shall return to that in the subsequent chapter. But even within the presuppositions of the Constantinian assumption it is pathetic when the churches continue to make themselves answerable to the dominant culture when it no longer is the center of power.

The truth is that those who constitute this social stratum are themselves victimized by the power of the technocratic structures of our society. These structures transcend the ability of men, individually or corporately, to direct them. They transcend, as we have already seen, even the chief technocrats—even presidents! And they transcend also that class which is supposed to be served by them.

In reality, the members of that class are themselves frightened and anxious little people. They are not any longer really able to believe in a world in which everything can be done, and by us. Their only real distinction from protesting groups, from the poor, from critical intellectuals, and from minority groups is that they cannot bring themselves to face the darkness that surrounds us all. They cannot face their own terrible impotence. More than the others, they suffer because they possess no frame of reference for reflection on the failure of the modern dream, the dream called "America."

Without doubt that is a significant distinction. Their whole world is falling apart, and they long since gave up any mythical, ideological, or religious grounds for

the contemplation of worlds falling apart. They can
only cope by repressing the knowledge of it, and by
carrying the dream to ever more absurd lengths. Thus
out of thin air they manufacture fantastic, surrogate,
unreal and plastic worlds, in which WASPs move back
into black neighborhoods, and presidents couldn't possibly be guilty of deceit, and death is sleep, and all
problems are soluble.

The Disney World is one of the more plastic enact-
ments of repressive positive thinking. The fact that it is
extremely popular—and lucrative—indicates something of the demand for such a world. The following
excerpts from an advertisement provide an excellent
explanation of that demand. A well-known airline is
offering to fly people to the real world of Walt Disney.
Their ad is written to seem as though a father was
reporting on the recent visit of the family to this amaz-
ing place:

> One of the biggest events of the day was about to hap-
> pen. A parade.
> Leading the procession were Mickey and Minnie Mouse,
> followed by several marching bands and dozens of other
> famous Disney characters. . . .
> Our children sat in amazement as President Lincoln got
> out of his chair. There before us was President Lincoln, as
> big as Life, speaking of the things that make countries
> great.
> As he sat down again, the star-filled sky behind him
> began to turn red. White clouds gathered and stretched
> across in bands, leaving a patch of blue at the upper left
> portion of the sky. . . .
> After the Hall of Presidents, the children wanted to see

Fort Wilderness where we got another glimpse of our great heritage.

We met and talked with a man there whose name was Del Rosengrant. A real blacksmith. . . .

We left civilization for a while after that and traveled on four famous rivers of the world.

The captain of our jungle boat safely guided us past hungry hippos, trumpeting elephants and spear-clutching headhunters. The kids really got a kick out of it and laughed aloud as my wife and I ducked from one of the elephants who threatened to squirt water at us.

Everyone who worked at Walt Disney World always seemed to be having as much fun as the visitors. And of course the grown-ups were all having as much fun as the children.

Walt Disney World was the kind of vacation our family will never forget. There was so much to see and experience. Together.

And then comes the punch line, printed in bold letters so it won't be missed by all the anxious people: How Your Children See the World Depends on What You Show Them.[72]

I remembered that I had shown my children Buchenwald. I also remembered that as we sat outside the Plötzensee Memorial in Berlin, while I told my young son about the courageous people who had been hanged there for resisting the Nazis, he began to cry and accused me: "Daddy, you tell me the most terrible things!"

There *are* terrible things, and there will be. And when a people determines to protect itself and its children from them, it is quite probable that that people will become the *cause* of terrible things.

The picture of life presented in the Disney World advertisement is no more offensive than the same picture presented in more refined and subtle ways. It is simply more obvious. In the Disney version the exaggeration of the dream becomes a *reductio ad absurdum*— patently unreal. Pure kitsch. Only those who want to be deceived can be deceived by it.

All our attempts at self-deceit are being unmasked today. Vietnam, the greatest of the recent attempts, backfired. We went there (or supported those who did) to show our innocent and nonpartisan championship of the good. We came away, not with honor, as it was said, but no longer really believing in honor. It isn't surprising that what followed next was the Watergate affair.

We are not in control, and we know it. The power has gone from us—from the dominant culture, from "Middle America," from . . . man. Presidents do not stand up and put everything to rights. Blacksmiths do not work merrily at their forges without thought of reward. Everybody does not have fun. Families do not always stay together—even when they play and pray together.

The continued identification of the churches with a social stratum that tries so pathetically to cling to the world view naïvely depicted by the Disney Corporation is not only pathetic. From the vantage point of a faith that sees a new potential for the gospel today, it is destructive. So long as the churches are bound up with that social stratum, they cannot be "there" for the people who are—and must be—more honest about what time it is. The unreality of the churches militates against the reality of the gospel.

Is there no way out? Is it possible to change this? Are the churches trapped in a cultural marriage of convenience? Are they bound to be a part of the plastic world, to cry "Peace, Peace," and to say that it is growing lighter? Or can they be delivered from the pursuit of unreality and become witnesses to the light that shines *in the darkness?*

Chapter 3

The Spirit to the Churches:
Disestablish Yourselves!

[handwritten: Read critically]

[handwritten: meaning of establishment?]

INTRODUCTION

WHAT IS REALLY REAL?

It isn't possible for all the churches in the world today to offer religious versions of the Disney World. Some have been denied that role. Here and there whole provinces of once-proud Christendom have been hurled into reality with a vengeance. The church in East Germany is a case in point.

Paul Kilborne offers the following vignette from the East German scene. It tells as much about the writer, an American Christian experiencing a different version of the church for the first time, as it tells about the church in that Marxist land. That makes it all the more appropriate for our present purposes.

It was Sunday and we were sitting in the old Marienkirche in Berlin, *Hauptstadt der D.D.R.* Some of my teachers had worshiped here when they were students. The great

*[handwritten: 1. The problem + the message
2. Implications of disestablishment
3. Freedom of disestablished church]*

church was almost full. Most of the people, I noticed, were young: students in parkas, bearded, many of them, and with long hair; young couples, some with children; single men and women in their early middle ages; and of course a generous sprinkling of "Omas," older women dressed in the sort of clothes I can remember, vaguely, from my early childhood and old movies. An elderly lady in my pew shared her hymnbook with me.

Just about the time the preacher commenced his sermon, the noise started up: mass bands of the *Freie deutsche Jugend* (Free German Youth) were playing in the square outside the church. We had seen them assembling there on our way in. Two or three hundred youngsters, and their directors and followers. They like to play on the steps of the great Television Tower, the landmark of contemporary East Berlin and showpiece of the Communist world.

The Television Tower! It shot up some 1200 feet into the sky. Looking at it, one had no doubt about its intention: surely it had been erected right alongside the old Marienkirche, and in the immediate vicinity of the bombed-out Berlin Cathedral, to proclaim the victory of the new society. "See!" it announces. "Just see for yourself how the new humanity of the socialist state towers over these dilapidated relics of the bourgeois-capitalist world." In a restaurant inside the sphere at the 600-foot level, you can have pie in the sky right now.

The same logic causes one to suspect that it is not just by chance that the mass bands of the *Freie deutsche Jugend* stage their concerts precisely at the time of service in the Marienkirche.

I had to move forward to hear the sermon. Even then it was necessary to strain my ears because of the noise of the bands. And I thought: "But maybe this is how it should be. Maybe one should always have to strain to hear sermons in churches. Anyway it would be more realistic. Because one way or another, the world is always there with its noise, its brassy choruses. And sometimes the tunes it plays are catchy."

"Test the spirits," the preacher was saying, "to see whether they be of God." And it seemed truer, more compelling . . . because it was so hard to hear.

Several months later I went again to the stately old Marienkirche. They were installing the new Bishop of East Berlin that Sunday, and the church was so full that I had to stand throughout the service, along with a hundred or more others. Again I was astonished at the youth of the congregation.

An unusual feature of this occasion was that a representative of the State had been sent. Officially, not incognito, as would be normal. He was sitting with other dignitaries in the chancel. One wondered what it meant.

Everyone waited eagerly for the sermon. What would the new bishop say? The bands weren't playing on this occasion, so it was possible for him to speak quietly and in an ordinary, friendly way.

"What is really real?" he asked.

Often what seems to be real turns out not to have been very real after all; while what seems unreal or insignificant shows up in a surprising light. Power turns out to have been weakness, and weakness power. What paraded itself as wisdom is unmasked as patent nonsense, and the foolishness of yesterday is revealed as truth and wisdom.

It is always difficult to tell what is really real. So much depends on one's perspective. Given the perspective of faith, it is sometimes possible to say with Paul that when we have been weak, then—precisely then!—we were strong. . . .

No word was said by way of relating this message to the political and cultural context. That wasn't necessary. Everybody knew what it meant, and how it might be applied, and what cheer it might give.

Afterward, I went out of the church and looked up at the

two towers: the old spire of the Marienkirche with its cross, and the Television Tower with its glass sphere and revolving restaurant, where you can have pie in the sky right now.

And for an instant it seemed to me that the *spire* was the higher of the two! The cross was towering over this shiney gadget of technological man. "In the cross of Christ I glory . . ."

I stepped back. I walked two hundred yards or so and looked again. Well of course the Television Tower was the loftier by far. Oh, there was no comparison! It towered for hundreds of feet above the spire. As I had known it did, all along.

Still, from a certain perspective . . .[73]

◆❧ 1 ❧◆

THE PROBLEM AND THE MESSAGE

Recapitulation: The Problem

I have begun this final chapter with a reference to the church in East Germany because that church stands out in my own experience, too, as a place from which "a certain perspective" can be gained. Christians in the German Democratic Republic have had to work out an alternative to the Constantinian arrangement. It is an exciting, provocative alternative; from it we can receive much help and encouragement in our own efforts to reform the churches.

Before I elaborate on that, it will be useful to recapitulate the argument of this study so far. I have described two conflicting experiences. They are shared by many Christians today, and also by a significant number of persons who would not call themselves Christians. I have labeled these experiences "the reality of the gospel" and "the unreality of the churches." The coming together of these two experiences is a source of great frustration for many of our contemporaries. Especially for thoughtful Christians but also for concerned human beings who are able to see in the Christian gospel something that could be pertinent to our human condition today.

It is frustrating to be caught between these two experiences. Not only do they conflict with each other but they cannot be kept nicely separate. The gospel is irrevocably bound up with the churches, and the churches with the gospel. Those who share these two experiences cannot avoid the conclusion that the unreality of the churches *stands in the way* of the new possibility of the gospel's being heard as somehow "real."

In other words, the unreality of the churches is not merely pathetic or ludicrous, something that one can commiserate or joke about with one's friends "afterward." It is a destructive, deadening thing. It undermines the prospect that at this critical juncture in time the Christian gospel could become a significant, constructive force in the struggle of man for survival, for civilization, for life.

So long as the churches constitute what Roman Catholic theologian Charles Davis called a "zone of untruth,"[74] the sense of falseness, vacuity, triviality, and unreality will cling to everything and everybody connected with them. So long as they are committed to obsolete world views and to strata of society that have their own questionable reasons for prolonging these

world views, it will be hard for Christians to enter into
the realities of the contemporary world. And it will be
equally difficult for sensitive, concerned persons of the
world to consider dialogue with Christians to be a significant undertaking.

Throughout this discussion I have been making an
important assumption, which I have nowhere tried to
cloak. Now I want to make it quite explicit and to
explain why it seems to me necessary. It is integral to
our whole understanding of the problem. I am referring to the assumption that, for better or worse, the
gospel *is* bound up with the churches.

Apart from this assumption, the problem I have been
describing here would not exist. Those who find the
Christian gospel meaningful for the human condition
today could simply go about their witness in the world
without a backward glance at the institutions called
churches. Some contemporary Christians have in fact
assumed that stance, though in my estimation it is,
finally, not a viable position to take. There are both
sociological and theological reasons for assuming an
inseparable connection between the Christian gospel
and the institutions that announce themselves as Christian churches.   *Reasons for*

In the first place, this connection is a sheer *sociological* *connection*
fact. Those who ignore it, who think it possible to have (1.)
the gospel unimpeded by association with the churches,
usually fool only themselves. Much of the so-called
"Christian underground," admirable as it is in many
respects, demonstrates the impossibility of an independent gospel. It tries to have a Christian message and life
unobstructed by the churches, but in actuality it is conscious of nothing so much as it is of the churches. The

shadow of institutional Christianity is cast upon all of its activity.

The sociological link between the gospel and the churches is simply a "given" of Christian experience, sometimes of bitter experience. Many have felt that as soon as they identify themselves as Christians, the whole weight of the ecclesiastical reputation for unreality falls upon them. A Christian layman who is a university professor once put it this way: "In the university you have to spend months, even years, convincing people that you aren't either a wild fundamentalist on the one hand or a bourgeois liberal on the other, before you can get down to honest relationships. As soon as they find out you're a Christian, you've acquired an image that you've really got to work at if you want to live it down!"

Perhaps that is why there is a strain of real bitterness running through the statements of the ex-pastors in the report to which I have referred. For many of these men, the unreality of the churches had become so pervasive that it could be escaped only by dropping everything— including faith itself. From many of those who retained their belief and tried to carry on some sort of Christian ministry in the world, one can detect a growing resentment of the ubiquitous church Christianity which, they feel, inhibits their witness.

In other words, it is simply difficult to dissociate Christian faith from the institutional forms in which it presents itself to society at large. It is at least as difficult as to divorce education from the institutions called schools.

In the second place, the assumption that the gospel is bound up with the churches grows out of *theological* reflection on the nature of the church. At this level the assumption becomes more difficult to express adequately. Perhaps I can avoid some of the difficulties, including the temptation to become too academically "theological," by stating the matter in quite personal terms.

If I found it possible on theological grounds to conclude that there is no relation whatsoever between the Christian gospel and the institutional churches; if I could simply identify the churches as religious or quasi-religious phenomena having nothing essential to do with Christianity, then I would certainly not worry about the inconsistencies between the gospel and ecclesiastical life. In spite of the sociological difficulties, I would simply forget about the churches and get on with my work as an interpreter of the gospel in the world today. Churchly unreality just would not constitute a problem for me.

But I cannot do that—alas! I cannot rid myself of the theological conviction that these churches of ours, for all their triviality and their pursuit of the unreal, are nevertheless implicated in the gospel. So it is not for me a matter of indifference whether or not they reflect that gospel or betray it. Try as I may, I cannot be nonchalant about them.

But how is one to understand this strange connection? It is by no means easy, and there are many pitfalls. Orthodox ecclesiasts of every color and denomination want to emphasize the inseparability of gospel and churches to such an extent that any radical critique of the churches from the side of the gospel is precluded. They insist that the gospel is the proclamation of Christ's church, and that Christ's church manifests itself visibly in the churches—or, more frequently, in some particular church. For them, the church of Jesus Christ is already realized in this or that denomination or ecumenical body.

It will be obvious that my assumption of a theological connection between gospel and churches does not run along these lines. That the gospel is the proclamation of the church of Jesus Christ is not in doubt. But that Christ's church is identifiable with the churches, all of them or one of them, *is* in doubt. It always has been— from the New Testament on. In fact, much of the New Testament is understandable only if it is seen in the light of just this doubt. This is especially so in the epistles. Moreover, the Protestant Reformers intended to make this continuing doubt about the relation between Christ's church and the churches a permanent aspect of Christian theology and practice. They realized from bitter experience that we must be wary of making an indelible connection between the church "visible" and the church "invisible." The Kingdom of Christ does not nicely coincide with church membership rolls. It is both broader and narrower.

On the other hand, there is another pitfall. It is possible to *use* the idea of the church's essential hiddenness and invisibility to escape responsibility for the all-too-visible churches. Thus the church becomes an ideal, forever unrealized in historical existence. Against this temptation, the cautioning words of Karl Barth are certainly appropriate:

> Take good note, that a parson who does not believe that in this congregation of his, including those men and women, old wives and children, Christ's own congregation exists,

does not believe at all in the existence of the Church. *Credo ecclesiam* means that I believe that here, at this place, in the visible assembly, the work of the Holy Spirit takes place.[75]

Such words can readily be used by ecclesiastical conservatism (as can so many of Barth's words!) to justify the ecclesiastical *status quo;* hence, to squelch all radical criticism of institutional Christianity. But surely that is not the point. The point is that the community that is formed around the gospel is, and must forever become, a *visible* community. Although it is the work of the Spirit, the church is not something ethereal or merely spiritual. To believe in the church means to believe that God's Word continues to make itself incarnate, to embody itself, to *real*-ize itself in the life of the world.

But this *real*-ization, this making *real*—what is it? It is not something that has happened once and for all, to be passed on from one generation to the next. It is not something static and permanently achieved. Rather, it is dynamic, always happening. It is, if you like, a process. But not a smooth and, so to speak, evolutionary process, as the word "process" invariably suggests. It is more like a struggle—an ongoing *r*evolution. Given the conditions of our fallen and recalcitrant humanity, the Spirit of God can impart the new reality of Christ to us only in the form of a continuous struggle with our spirits (Rom. 8:15 f.).

As for us, we are afraid to be made real. We cling to the old reality that we call life—our "way of life." We resist identity with the man of the cross. That can only seem like death to us. And so it is—death to what we call life. Thus our incorporation into the reality of the body of Christ can occur only as we are confronted again and

again by divine judgment *against* our surrogate reality.
Again and again we have to be cast into the darkness in
order to see that the light we have been relying on is
ersatz light. Again and again we have to be subjected to
the really unnerving recognition that our houses are
built on sand. Again and again we have to hear the
prophetic and critical gospel, which recalls us to "what
is really real."

"need for "feeling"

If this is what the redemptive process is like, then it
is not necessary to exclude the churches from this process. Their very penchant for trivia, their almost deliberate pursuit of unreality, even their attempts to bury
the gospel by identifying it with a cultural ideology—
all this somehow fits the description of what happens to
those who are singled out for hearing this "good news."
It can be seen, all of it, as a habitual and very human
flight from the new reality into which the Spirit of God
strives to bring us. Perhaps the characteristic mark of
the churches, from the New Testament on, is just this
flight from reality. Whoever has a good grasp of the
story of the people of God as it is told in both Testa-
ments would not be surprised at such a suggestion. In
the Bible, God is always trying to give his people *real*
(Jesus said "abundant") life. For their part, the people
are always exchanging it for some mess of pottage or
other.

That the churches are unreal today is therefore not
astonishing. It is even somehow within the apostolic
tradition—that is, the tradition of Peter who denied,
of Judas who betrayed, of the whole lot of them when
they vied with one another for power and promi-
nence, when they forsook him and fled, when they
went back to their fishing nets, when they didn't

really understand what it was all about.

But the other side of this process is that <u>Jesus Christ will not abandon his people to the unreality they seek</u>. That too is what is meant by the promise that "the gates of hell shall not prevail against it"—against "my church" (Matt. 16:18). Triumphal, power-seeking Christendom has always taken this as celestial guarantee of its victory over all worldly rivals. But there is a threat in this promise. Christ defends his church not only from the hell that is outside it but from the far more insidious evil that is within. He will defend it from the hellish internal fear of being made real, from the mediocrity that is neither hot nor cold, from the banality and conformism that is always looking about for bushels to hide the light under, from the deviousness that pursues false scandals so as to evade the scandal of the cross. This is the judgment that "begins at the household of God."

In short, the <u>fundamental theological connection</u> between the <u>gospel and the churches</u> is nothing more nor less than the <u>faithfulness</u> of God. He will continue to re-form the churches by the judging power of the gospel. He will not cease calling into being a representative, priestly people out of "no people" (Rom. 4:17). He will always seek to create the church out of the churches. The church will always be, more or less, a creation out of nothing (*creatio ex nihilo*).

All the same, the creating God of the gospel does not engage in this judging/edifying work strictly, so to speak, from above. We are not dealing with a *deus ex machina*, who swoops in from heaven at the point of greatest difficulty and sets everything right. We are dealing with a God who "moves in a mysterious way,

His wonders to perform." For our present concern, this means that he seems to perform this tearing-down and building-up work in the churches, <u>normally, from within.</u>

Thus when the writer of the Apocalypse sends off his searing letters to the seven churches (Rev., chs. 2;3) there can be no doubt that the judgment is God's: "Hear what the Spirit says to the churches." But they themselves are given the grace to participate in this judgment against them. They must penetrate through the layers of unreality and mere appearance ("you have the name of being alive") and discern the bitter truth underneath ("and you are dead"). Upon *them* is laid the responsibility for repentance and reform.

The Message — <u>an</u> answer or <u>the</u> answer?

The conclusion cannot be avoided, I think, that in the churches today we have a difficult but absolutely essential task laid upon us. It has been virtually thrust upon us—all of us who remain within the churches. All of us would prefer it otherwise. We are not at all equipped for it. But it must be done all the same, and by us: by this generation.

For if the life *of the churches* is such that it is proving to be the stumbling block to belief for many sensitive Christians and non-Christians, then <u>surely this false scandal has to be removed.</u> If the unreality of our churchly pursuits and preoccupations stands in the way of the reality and potential power of the gospel, then obviously something will have to be done about the churches.

The question is, What?

Many agree that something has to be done. Many are

indeed doing something. Some of what is being done is, no doubt, significant. Some of it, on the other hand, is a little like the sort of housekeeping that moves dirt from one corner to another. No one, however, could accuse our generation of Christendom of being short on ideas for change. Our heads are dizzy with such affirmations, plans, strategies, and programs.

But my intention is to reflect on the question What? at a level that seems to me more elementary than plans and programs. For whatever reason, most of our plans and programs appear to me to neglect altogether this more elementary level. For all the vaunted radicalism of some of them, sweeping away this or introducing that, they almost invariably propose to continue on the same foundation. That is, they nearly always assume that the churches can continue only on the basis of the Constantinian arrangement, however interpreted. Normally this is simply *assumed*, not acknowledged. Moreover, one has the distinct impression that most of the Change-makers are not even aware of the assumption.

If our aim is the perpetuation of the churches, then no doubt the Constantinian assumption *must* be invoked. But why, in the first place, should the perpetuation of the churches be our aim? Surely the only authentic goal for faith is that, for the sake of the world, the gospel should be heard. If the churches as they stand are getting in the way of that hearing, then their *continuation* is the very last thing Christian faith should hope for. All that could then legitimately be hoped for would be their *transformation*, that is, that they might become true witnesses to the world-redeeming gospel.

If once we could get our priorities straight, if once and for all we could grasp that what comes first is the gospel, then we should have a perspective from which to entertain the more elementary change that is habitually overlooked by the Change-makers. If only we could rid ourselves of the hidden presupposition that above all what must be sustained are the churches, we would be in a position to hear the most rudimentary word of the church's Lord: namely, that *it is time to dispense altogether with the Constantinian assumption.*

Hear what the Spirit says to the churches of the Western world: "Disestablish yourselves!" I doubt if the Spirit of God has ever spoken so clearly to the churches about anything.

The churches of North America are singled out for special mention in this summons of the Spirit of God because our form of Establishment is particularly insidious. More important than that, it is possible that our deliberate "disestablishment" could mean something highly significant not only for this continent but for the rest of the world that is oppressed by the sort of world view possessed by the dominant culture of this continent.

What might it mean for the poor and oppressed of the Third World, what might it mean for the enemies of the West, what might it mean for the other religions of the world, and for the ecumenical church, if in our time the Christian churches of North America began to say and do things radically different from the dominant culture, the Establishment? What if it happened that people all over the globe began to learn that within North America—this home of multinational corporations, this continent which consumes 44 percent of the world's resources—a people existed, albeit a minority, who resisted all of that *in the name of Jesus Christ?*

To be sure, there are already voices of Christians on this continent who can be heard in other parts of the world saying and doing just this. But should we be content with gaining our credibility as churches through those voices? Do those voices obviate the necessity that is laid upon all of us, upon our institutions? Surely not! The Spirit speaks *to the churches,* not only to individuals here and there. He calls Christian ministers to bid their congregations, "Disestablish yourselves!" He calls congregations to require of their presbyteries, synods, conferences, and head offices, "Disestablish yourselves!" And each man among those who remain within the churches is called to teach his brother, "Disestablish yourself!"

Much more than words and teaching is involved in the disestablishment of Christianity. In the first place it is necessary for as many of us as can bear it to understand what it means to a large minority in our society to regard the churches as an integral part of the Establishment. We will not be in a position to disestablish ourselves as churches until we have grasped the fact and character of our establishment.

For us in North America, that is in itself difficult enough. To date, only a few have seemed capable of comprehending the subtle kind of establishment that we have here. Even when it is comprehended, it is hard to know how to act in obedience to the command of the Spirit that we disestablish ourselves. It is one thing to disengage Christianity from economic, political, and legal moorings. It is something else again to disentangle faith from its cultural moorings; to distinguish between the gospel and the ideology of the dominant culture of our society.

Civil religion again

No wonder I can't quite separate the two yet! all tangled!

Many of those who have an inkling of what the Spirit says to the churches feel almost intuitively that it could not be done. In a real sense, this fatalism infects us all. We are discouraged at the prospects for the churches in any case. Yet we think, perhaps secretly, that as individuals, as a generation, we may be able to sneak through for a few more years on the old, Christendom pattern. History is giving us a little grace. Perhaps we can continue to be ministers along the usual lines. Perhaps congregations, presbyteries, conferences, synods, teachers of theology, Sunday schools, head offices, and bishops can go on along the usual lines. Perhaps history will not close in on us entirely.

If we really must change so drastically, let us wait for history to do that. Maybe the Spirit of God *is* calling us to disestablish ourselves; but in the meantime there are endowments from the past, from the "old families," and there are services to be conducted, weddings to perform, and funerals—well, who would look after the funerals? Also, the world has become accustomed to the face of the Christian Establishment. Is it not still glad enough to have us around to do the religious thing: to bless its various enterprises, its banquets, its parliamentary deliberations, its presidential breakfasts, its wars . . . ?

So we comfort ourselves with the thought that while the Spirit of God may be calling upon us to make this astonishing alteration, time permits us a little respite from the Spirit's command.

Does it?

Surely all of this is pure rationalization. No doubt it is understandable and human enough. But it is, all the same, nonsense. Time only appears to give us a little period of grace. The fact is, we *are being* disestablished. The only respite that time is giving us—and it is certainly not going to be very long!—is time enough for us to answer the question: "Will you *be* disestablished, or will you *disestablish yourselves?*"

The character of our disestablishment, as well as the fate of the future church among us, greatly depends on which of these alternatives we choose.

It is clear enough what lies behind our hesitation and rationalization. It is fear. Fear that we would not be up to it. Fear of giving up our supposed status as clergy and congregations and denominations (a status that we don't *really* have anyway!). Fear of the risk involved. Fear of leaving the fleshpots of Egypt. Fear of the wilderness.

Fear of the Exodus

Out of this fear, we experience the end of Christendom as a catastrophe. Everything is falling apart. Churches closing, congregations lethargic and dwindling, seminaries struggling to keep going. We do have some money in the bank still; but it isn't increasing, and most of us are drawing on the capital by now.

What we need—and badly—is a vision of the *possibilities* inherent in the disestablished situation. The end of Christendom is not a tragedy. Indeed, it could be the beginning of the church.

The Message Exemplified

What is so heartening about the church in East Germany today? In it, one can see the message of the Spirit to the churches exemplified. The result is not tragedy. It is a wonderful new beginning of life.

In East Germany a church that has disestablished itself is able, just *because* it is disestablished, to exist in that gray world in something like New Testament terms. It is a light in the midst of the gloomy, humorless, bureaucratic, and slogan-ridden official society; a pinch of salt in a plate of otherwise insipid fare; a bit of yeast in a loaf that without it would be flat indeed!

We may as well recognize that the church in the German Democratic Republic was hardly so courageous and imaginative as to take upon itself its own disestablishment. On the contrary, there were many who could not accept the disestablishment, even when it was thrust upon them by the powers that be. There still are a few. They could not imagine the church of Jesus Christ in a disestablished situation, an alien and officially unwanted people. Many of those who vehemently rejected such an image of the church are now in the West. A few, embittered, remain.

Yet those who have given leadership in the East German church, and who have molded it in its present style, have done so for just the reason I have referred to above: they saw in the *necessity* of disestablishment an *opportunity*. Instead of protesting, instead of holding out for some revised version of the usual Constantinian arrangement, instead of biding their time and depending on Western aid and deliverance, they heeded the command of the Spirit and sought another route altogether.

Concretely this is what that meant. Against those within and those outside its own ranks who turned to the West and wished nothing but ill for the Communists, the church in East Germany under the guidance of people such as Johannes Hamel of Naumburg took its stand *within* the Marxist world. I don't mean that it blessed Communism—that is a stupid charge that is sometimes made by Western Christians. To bless Communism in that context would have been nothing more nor less than a pursuance of the old Constantinian line: try to get power by latching onto the *new* source of power. In this case, anyway, there was no possibility of courting influence with power, for the power is by definition opposed to the Christian religion.

To decide for life in the Communist state meant, rather, to decide for a disestablished role for the church. That is, it meant to decide *against* being present in that society as an official element of the society. But the other side of that decision *against* was a decision *for*: namely, to be there *for* the men, women, and children of that state. Just because it couldn't be and didn't have to be there as an official element in the society, it could be there *for the people* of that society in a new way.

To put it in terms of the Scriptural metaphor used throughout this study, the church in East Germany discovered that it could now be present for Nicodemus. Even if Nicodemus turned out to be a Marxist—even a doctrinaire Marxist, quite basically and officially opposed to the gospel.[76]

The new possibility of Christian presence in the disestablished situation is a theme of much of the literature coming out of East Germany and other Marxist lands today. It is to be heard, for example, in this statement from Hamel's *A Christian in East Germany:*

> You understand that because of this gospel every day takes away from us the hope we have from the West, and we allow it to be taken. We experience how God's living word makes bound men here and now so free that they begin and end the day with his praise. Therefore, they are free

throughout each day to take the steps required by sober understanding of it, without being a slave to the question: "What will happen tomorrow?" God has something in mind for these Communists whom no one wishes any good and no one trusts to do anything good.

We are privileged to be there when he works and to be used by this grace. Our one concern is that we not resist what God is doing, not that we be relieved from our task by bombs and tanks. For "it is a great thing to live in the East Zone." My wife and I say that sometimes, in different tones of voice: now questioning, now bitter, now despairing or scornful, but ever again joyful. The old Adam would often prefer it otherwise and he looks every morning towards the West. But the joyful message of God himself points us back to the living people here, and makes it clear to us that he has given up no single one of them. Why should the Communists be lost? There is, to be sure, a sin unto death, for which we are asked to pray no longer. But why should we be weary of the repentance of many among whom God himself is continually at work.[77]

These are not the words of Constantinian Christianity. It is not accidental that they should sound so close to the New Testament at many points.

It is no easy route that the church in East Germany has been called to walk. It is the old Via Dolorosa, the Way of the Cross, that the church knew in its earliest years and at a few points throughout its history. There are no dramatic persecutions, as occurred to confessing Christians under Hitler. But the steady strain of pressure to conform, not to pay the price of a different witness and life, is in many ways more difficult to endure than outright persecution.

A man like Johannes Hamel, for example, who has identified with the men and women of the new society, must nonetheless as a Christian suffer the rejection of the very people he wants to help. Officially, no man in East Germany may be so "suspect" by the powers that be as is Hamel. The Party prefers that Christians be predictably conservative, bourgeois, and West-oriented.

Again, the children of pastors are not permitted to go to the university. In villages and towns it is dangerous or compromising to be too closely associated with the church. Especially is this so for men whose work depends on faithfulness to Party ideals or at least nonresistance.

In faculties of theology there are normally professors of Marxism-Leninism. These persons are virtually heads of their faculties, and their colleagues feel accountable to them. Besides, there are always informers in classes, and the professor who steps outside the strictly defined limits of his subject can expect trouble. For example, it would be going beyond the boundaries of the study of theology to make any comparison between Marxist and Christian interpretations of man and history. In East Germany nothing comparable to the pre-1968 Prague dialogue between Christianity and Marxism is permitted or even thinkable.

The attempt is clearly to relegate Christianity to the status of an antiquated, almost-defunct tradition, totally irrelevant to the life of the contemporary world. It is carried so far as to screen Christian literature carefully, and to remove anything that might sound "advanced." Thus Paul Kilborne reports that in one seminary that he had visited several times, all the books of Paul Tillich and Reinhold Niebuhr (among many others) had been removed from the shelves. An officer of the state had inspected the library, and a few weeks later a list of books arrived with the warning that the seminary would be closed down if these books were not removed. They were put into the crypt of the chapel.

The churches of East Germany are poor. Ministers are poor, by our standards. The temptation is always present either to give it all up and join the official society or to flee to the West. Seventeen millions, half the population, have fled since this state began.

Yet I can add my testimony to that of many other Western Christians who have had the privilege of coming to know the church in East Germany. Never have I experienced so much *reality* in the church! Suddenly it seems that the whole thing—the gospel, the Christian life, the two-thousand-year-old tradition—is true, real! The New Testament comes to life. Of course I don't mean that one is able to overlook the difference between Paul's time and ours. But at least the words of Paul and other New Testament writers don't ring false there. One can hear the New Testament read in worship there and not be embarrassed by the discrepancy between what it says about and to Christians and the way we are in our congregations.

> For consider your call, brethren; not many of you were wise according to worldly standards, not many were powerful, not many were of noble birth; but God chose what is foolish in the world to shame the wise, God chose what is weak in the world to shame the strong. (I Cor. 1:26 f.)

Or this:

> For I think that God has exhibited us apostles as last of all, like men sentenced to death; because we have become a spectacle to the world, to angels and to men. We are fools for Christ's sake. (I Cor. 4:9 f.)

Or from the tradition of Peter:

> Beloved, do not be surprised at the fiery ordeal which comes upon you to prove you, as though something strange were happening to you. But rejoice in so far as you share Christ's sufferings. (I Peter 4:12 f.)

Or from the tradition of Jesus:

> Blessed are you when men revile you and persecute you and utter all kinds of evil against you falsely on my account. (Matt. 5:11.)

These are not *unusual* utterances from the Scriptures; they are the normal descriptions of the church. In the established situation, which is to say during the greater share of its long history, the church could receive such statements as these only by falsifying either the Bible or its own life. It is nothing short of ludicrous when a rich, well-dressed, and eminently respectable congregation sits quietly in the midst of luxury while one of its own reads such passages as these out of the New Testament. It is the stuff out of which great irony is made!

Not incidentally, if we are looking for the roots of the churches' unreality, we should consider this point too. I mean the astonishing, really shocking discrepancy between what is said in our primary Sourcebook about the Christian congregation and the Christian life and, on the other hand, what actually transpires in our church services and among Christian congregations in the world. A child easily senses this discrepancy. We now have the experience of at least one whole generation of children who have sensed it so strongly that they cannot endure it.

In the disestablished situation that one finds in East Germany it is the young, chiefly, who turn to the church for something authentic, true, real. They are seeking an alternative to the official world that is kept going, as all official worlds are, by propaganda.

It is calculated, for example, that there are well over a thousand students of Protestant theology in the German Democratic Republic. Many of them study theology, not for the sake of getting jobs as ministers, but because it offers some sort of alternative to the official *educational* line.

The young seek out the church for an alternative life-style, too: something with color in it, and the possibility of honest talk, friendship, and just plain fun! They come in great numbers for meetings of the *Studentengemeinde* (equivalent to our Student Christian Movement) in universities. And with some danger to themselves, at that.

It is not yet necessary for the church in East Germany to be an "underground" in the sense of the early church. The right of assembly is given to it—but for two purposes only: worship and Bible study. Apparently the State felt that it had nothing to fear from these activities. In view of the churches' performance over the past few centuries one must grant that the State's conclusion in this case was entirely realistic! But in the disestablished situation, many things that might have been perfectly innocuous, such as the Bible, worship, meetings of church synods and committees, the study of theology, the offices of pastor, chaplain, theological

*Ho ho!
and how
sad!*

professor, take on new meanings.

The reason for it is quite simple: *the whole thing becomes credible once more*. Christianity becomes consistent with *a – ha!* its roots.

Christianity was born in the situation of disestablishment. It would be hard to conjure up anything less "established" than the cross and the community that formed around it. Whenever Christianity has become part of the established order, it has exhibited at least a certain hypocrisy in relation to its own roots. Usually what it has demonstrated has been far more serious than hypocrisy; often it has been nothing less than a betrayal of Christ himself, who keeps turning up on the side of the disestablished and dispossessed.

It would be a mistake to say that Christianity belongs, on the contrary, to that which is *against* the Establishment. Always, in every culture, the protest movement *Important* resists those in authority and tries to undermine their power. To bind the church perennially to the Counter Establishment is just as absurd as to bind it to the Establishment. It belongs to neither. It belongs to Christ. It follows his Way[78]; and that Way precludes identification with ideologies of every sort. It is a flexible Way, and one for which very little direction can be given in advance. It may turn in this direction or in that. Who knows where one may be carried as he follows this Way of the Christ? (Cf. John 21:18.) The Way must be open, bound neither to right nor left, free to walk with either. Certainly the church has to move through time and make friends with strangers of many sorts, including also many strange ideologies. It dare not sigh and use its freedom to keep aloof from . . . politics!

But it *is* free—bound to Christ, and therefore not to

men's ways of life. Free, not for its own sake, but for the sake of God's beloved world—"God's beloved East Zone" (Hamel). If it resists identification with either those who rule or those who resist, it is not for its own comfort, but because it is vigilant for man. Man's needs are never the same. One day Adam may have fallen into a ditch, the victim of thieves; the next he may have become one of the thieves! So the Way of the Christ must of necessity be open—the antithesis of being doctrinaire. It is open, not because the Christ is fickle, unstable, or unpredictable as the leader along this Way. It is open because he is following after the lost one, man. Even Christ does not know in advance what direction this strangely free, strangely bound creature will take.

In East Germany, the church has formed itself again in response to this Way. It is not so much institution as it is movement. It tries to respond to the movement of its Lord, who is himself moving. He moves always farther into the unknown places of this new society, always deeper into its grayness and its night, because Nicodemus is there.

※ 2 ※

THE IMPLICATIONS OF DISESTABLISHMENT

Disestablishment as Opportunity

Could we not take courage from the East German as well as from other numerous instances of the disestablished situation present in the contemporary world: in K. H. Ting's China, in Gutiérrez' Latin America, in South Korea where an authoritarian Right threatens humanity and freedom? Could we not also explore the Way as an alternative to Christendom, movement as an alternative to institution? Must we really wait until there are no choices left for us, no way for us to *choose* the mode of our disestablishment? Could we not now (but already it is very late!) disestablish *ourselves?*

No doubt a great many people in our churches are quite unprepared to hear such counsel. Some would not even comprehend it. Others, who comprehend it well enough, reject it out of hand—a priori.

These latter will argue that since we have these privileges and rights, these positions of influence, these opportunities for service, also these exemptions and honors, we should not relinquish them but *make the best use of them.*

Sometimes this position can seem persuasive. Its advocates know well how to justify what may be questionable means by accenting the desirable ends these means could serve. Could we not, they ask, instead of giving up the power we have because of our sixteen-century-old *modus operandi* with Caesar—could we not, instead, determine to put the benefits of this arrangement to better use? Let us use our influence with riches and power to improve the condition of the poor, the handicapped, the aged, the French, political protest groups, homosexuals—and some would even go so far as to add racial minorities.

Over against these attractive proposals there always stands the great weight of evidence. Having had such possibilities for centuries, the churches have by no means exploited them *in that way*. Besides, such proposals usually represent little more than stopgap thinking. At one level, one can only agree with their sentiments.

It is just and noble to use whatever influence we have with power to free the oppressed and to help the needy. But doing such things does not represent an *alternative* to Christendom. It does not meet the challenge of the Spirit that we find quite another way of being in the world than the way of seeking power by proximity to power.

Besides those who could not comprehend the challenge to disestablishment, and those who comprehend it but reject it, there is still another group in whom I have special interest. These are people who grasp the necessity of disestablishment—some can even become excited by the opportunities for developing an alternative to the Christendom experience of the church. But then, like the seeds in Christ's parable that fell into shallow earth, in the day-to-day life of the churches, where such opportunities would have to be worked out, they become afraid and practical. The deadly momentum of institutional Christianity carries them along with it. They conclude in their hearts that the search for a new way of being the church may be exciting, but that it cannot work. Not here. Not now. Now among *us*.

it's safer + secure

This sort of resignation seems to me rather pervasive among us. Younger clergy, who as students or through exposure to something vital in world or church were grasped by a vision of what the church might be in the contemporary world, so often capitulate to maintaining what is. I can think of dozens of my fellow students, and of my own students, who have since become pretty much like the clergy they once despised and rejected. And I know that I myself could rightly be seen by them as having fallen prey to the same inevitabilities. We

must not be!

retain some memory of the vision. It haunts us and often makes us dissatisfied with what we are and what we do, but we lack the courage to act upon it. Anyway, we are not convinced that it could make a difference if we did.

Caution takes hold of us; and caution is strongly bolstered by growing responsibilities and commitments in our personal lives. We know of many who one way or another have acted, as they thought, in accordance with such a vision. Sometimes their acts are altogether admirable, and we are stirred to guilt by them. But many of these acts have been clumsy, abortive, pathetic, and sometimes foolish—deeds that gained nothing either for the church or for the individuals concerned. These observations increase our natural caution. Why should we play the fool, when it might easily turn out that we were not being "Christ's fool" but just the damn fool?

We live, in the meantime, with the vague or sometimes acute consciousness that the old Christendom order of things is going to topple one of these days. And each of us who makes his living in some sort of professional ministry today lives with the sense that he just might not be able to finish the work he began under the same relatively secure conditions. I wonder how many clergy today ask themselves, with some degree of anxiety, whether they would be fitted for any other kind of work should that become necessary.

All the same, most of us are prepared to carry on "business as usual." We adjust to the omega that looms on the horizon, and tell ourselves that it will happen when it happens. When it happens, we will respond with whatever genius we can muster. Meanwhile, as the Scriptures say, "Sufficient unto the day is the evil thereof." The trouble is, it *is happening!*

So many of us seem to have a sort of catastrophic view of history. One day "it" will happen. The churches of old Christendom will all close their doors, and the clergy will all take off their collars (or whatever else we have put on as symbols of our neutrality) and "it" will have happened.

In some parts of the world something like that has occurred. In East Germany, for example. Overnight, almost, the centuries-old Christendom situation was replaced by one in which the church was once again only barely licit.

But the disestablishment that we face in the Western nations is one that comes from structures far more subtle than were operating in postwar East Germany. In our scenario, Christendom is not being pushed out by a big bang. It is going out with a scarcely audible whimper. We will not have understood the whimper until we have grasped the fact that part of it is our very indecisiveness, our resignation, our waiting for something to be done *to* us.

Behind this resignation lies the almost indelible sense, instilled in us by centuries of Christian triumphalism, that there really is no alternative to Constantinian Christendom. The death of Christendom means, in fact, the death of Christianity. Hence, we can only witness the dwindling numbers, the loss of prestige and influence, the closing of buildings, and the decrease of financial assets with sadness and a sense of loss. We are sometimes quite demoralized by it all.

But it is loss only so long as we continue to think within the framework of the Christendom mentality. If once we can grasp something of the possibilities that can come to the Christian community in the situation of disestablishment—*and only in that situation*—then we shall begin to understand the truth of the matter. What is from one side the *command* of the Spirit of God is from the other the *permission* and the grace to do something truly significant. To do it! Not to wait for it to be done to us.

The truth is that we are not victims of a catastrophic or pathetic necessity. We are the recipients of an opportunity. It is indeed an opportunity which some of the best and greatest of our forefathers in faith longed to have and were not granted. For the most faithful Christians have always known, deep in their bones, that Constantine's gift to the church, raising it to the level of an official religious cult, was never anything but a very mixed blessing. Not even in the best of times. Mostly, it was more like a betrayal. I frankly doubt very much that Jesus ever imagined his church in terms of an official religion of a whole civilization. I just do not believe the idea ever crossed his mind. He was thinking of a little flock, a pinch of salt, a bit of yeast, a witnessing community. And I suspect even more strongly that Paul, if he had been alive at the time of the Edict of Milan, would have opposed it with all his might!

He too knew that "power corrupts," and that proximity to power corrupts, and that absolute proximity to power corrupts absolutely! On the contrary, his notion was: When we are weak, then we are strong.

Instead of fear and the sense of loss, then, we might expend some of our psychic and intellectual energy today in the churches reflecting on the power of weakness. Instead of this pervasive, barely suppressed mourning that one senses among many Christians to-day, we might give serious thought to the possibilities inherent in littleness.

Power of weakness

Karl Rahner puts it succinctly:

> When we say that we have the right to make a cool, dispassionate reckoning with the fact that the church is a *diaspora*, we mean, understanding it rightly, the very opposite of resignation and defeatism. If we once have the courage to give up our defence of the old facades which have nothing or little behind them; if we cease to maintain, in public, the pretence of a universal Christendom; if we stop straining every nerve to get *everybody* married in the church and onto our registers (even when success means only, at bottom, a victory for tradition, custom and ancestry, not for true faith and interior conviction); if, by letting all this go, we visibly relieve Christianity of the burdensome impression that it accepts responsibility for everything that goes on under this Christian top-dressing, the impression that Christianity is *natura sua* a sort of Everyman's Religious Varnish, a folk-religion (at the same level as that of folk-costumes)—*then* we can be free for real missionary adventure and apostolic self-confidence.

If we could relinquish this ancient ambition of Christendom to possess all, says Rahner, we would be delivered from the depressing experience of watching what we regard as our "possessions" dwindle. Certainly we must continue to believe that *God* has designs on the whole creation. Certainly we may confess that *he* wills to have all mankind.

> But we cannot say that he is doing so only if we, meaning the Church, have everybody. Why should we not today alter to our use, quite humbly and dispassionately, a saying of St. Augustine's: Many whom God has, the Church does

not have; and many whom the Church has, God does not have?[79]

Disengaging Christianity *from* Ideology

The disestablishment of Christianity entails both a negative and a positive thrust. Or, in other words, it means a twofold application of the concept of freedom: freeing *from* something, and freeing *for* something. As always, it is not possible to separate this twofold application of freedom *in practice*. But it is perhaps necessary to separate it for purposes of discussion. First, I shall discuss what I think is involved in the disestablishment of Christianity as a "freeing *from*."

There are two aspects in this negative thrust, this freeing of authentic Christianity from what is not essential to it. First, it must entail a disengagement of Christian faith from the cultural or ideological framework in which it has become entwined. That is the primary *theological* task of disestablishment. Secondly, it must entail a relinquishing of the Constantinian assumption altogether. And that is the primary *ethical* or *political* task.

As we have argued here, Establishment in the North American context has been first and foremost a *cultural* phenomenon. Christianity has been identified with the highest virtues and values of our culture at large. Consequently the most important work of disestablishment on this continent has to concern itself with the theological task of disengaging authentic Christian faith from the ideology that has informed our "American" experience.

What is called for is a serious, rigorous, and relentless examination of the ways in which Christian belief has been ideologically misused—that is, used to support and propagate ideas, values, goals, and mores that are not strictly consistent with the gospel of Jesus Christ.

Such an examination has implications for both the study and the practical life of serious Christians.

At the level of study, it means a concentrated effort to expose ourselves to the Biblical, patristic, Reformation, and other special sources of Christian belief. We need to do this, not only as students of the past, but as people who recognize who *we* are and what *we*, as representatives of this North American culture, bring with us to the interpretation of these sources. We are a people who realize that we have our hidden agendas and that our forefathers also had theirs. Because we are who we are, we *expect* to find in these Christian sources religious confirmation of our cultural assumptions: the supremacy of the male, the sacredness of work, the rectitude of economic capitalism, the condemnation of homosexuality, etc. Beyond that, we are looking for divine sanction of even more rudimentary concepts of our culture such as the call of man to master the natural environment; the confirmation of the idea of historical progress; the affirmation of our official optimism, our "pursuit of happiness."

We may no longer assume that we are free of these biases and downright prejudices. We are called upon to expose to ourselves and our neighbors the extent to which these cultural and ideological presuppositions have influenced our interpretation of the Bible and of the whole Christian tradition. We have heard the stories of the Old Testament and the parables of Jesus in the way that we have largely because there are certain things we wanted to hear in them—and certain things we did not want to hear! After all, whenever we have tried to draw the portrait of Jesus graphically, we have usually depicted him without Jewish features at all! Why should we not suppose that the same principle is at work in our theology and our Biblical interpretation?

The disengagement of Christianity from the ideology of the WASP must begin with *such* study. I know it is *l.b.cont'd* folly to imagine that serious and frank study of this sort will be undertaken by more than a minority within the churches. That objection is really beside the point.

In the first place, the only element within the present constituency of the churches that will be able to withstand the subtle pressures of the slow demise of Christendom consists of the ones who are able to "give a reason for the hope that is in [them]." Reasons cannot be given without serious study and reflection. So it is by no means insignificant today to concentrate on "minorities" within the churches—in this case, the few who can discipline themselves to honest study.

Moreover, we ought not immediately to lament that such study is beyond ordinary laymen. Something interesting has been happening in our time that can be a great psychological and methodological boon to this kind of study. Various groups and movements have sprung up all over the world, mostly representative of minorities. These groups have made all of us conscious of the hidden assumptions that we bring to daily life and conversation. As a result, there is a climate of thought in which to raise the question of ideological prejudice in relation to Bible study. It can be more easily grasped by ordinary laymen today than might have been the case formerly.

A people who have *begun* to realize that there are

hidden assumptions in their speech and their practices that are deeply injurious to blacks, Indians, homosexuals, women, and others are perhaps in a better position than before to realize that they may be reading and using the Bible to support quite unbiblical concepts.

I.b. (cont'd)

Another immeasurable bonus that we now possess for such an undertaking is the real presence of the ecumenical church, particularly the churches of the Third World. These churches are of special significance to us because they have been casting off their earlier subordination to North Atlantic Christianity. In place of subordination to the "Mother" churches of the European–North American world, the churches of the Third World have developed an indigenous theological posture. They have learned how to read and how to tell the Story out of their own experience. They have therefore become highly critical of their "founding" churches in Europe and North America, which had given them the Story in such a way that Jesus had to be a white man! They are sharp, these Christians of Asia, Africa, and South America. They are not at all sentimental about their "Mother" churches. They do not mind stepping on our toes.

In fact, it becomes increasingly obvious that their main message to the maternal churches is not a little hostile. It has to be. In Christian obedience they, the *Christians* of the Third World, have identified with *their* people. And most of *their* people are the victims of *our* people! And of us.

So their insistence that we read the Bible again and try to get it straight this time—try to get it disentangled from the kind of imperialism that has informed our affluent Western world—is entirely sincere. They are

standing behind us as we engage in this study. As a
Western Christian theologian I can feel them looking
over my shoulder today. They are very, very curious to
know how we in North America and in Europe will
acquit ourselves as Christians in identifying who we are
in this domain of the oppressors.

Beyond study, which is basic to the work of disestablishment, the disengagement of Christianity from its
Western ideological matrix must involve innumerable
practical matters in the daily life of the churches. Here
I can only be suggestive. Some of the things that could
be included at this point have already been mentioned
or implied in other places. We must decide once and for
all to rid ourselves of the idea that everybody belongs
to us; that all must be baptized, married, and buried by
us. We must renounce our overwillingness to function
as a folk religion, blessing banquets and wars without
question, praying over ships and sealing wax, cabbages
and kings!

In our North American context, I think that cultural
disestablishment would have to mean especially a consistent and courageous determination *not* to allow ourselves to be moved, always, in directions amenable to
that dominant culture to which we have been wedded.
A determination, in other words, to be on the watch lest
we be used by "Middle America."

Precisely how the churches can be freed from the
sheer political, economic, and psychic *hold* of the dominant culture is a problem that can only be worked out
in practical deeds undertaken in the heat of each day's
evil. The first step toward resolution is to recognize—
through the sort of study proposed above—that we do
possess this bias, that we "listen" more carefully for

what the doctors, lawyers, and merchant chiefs of our congregations are calling for than we do for the priorities of the poor who are on the periphery of our churches. Or let us say more honestly: the poor and all the others who are *not* inside the churches just *because* the doctors, lawyers, and merchant chiefs are so influential in them.

For the clergy, disestablishment at this level of practical, daily life will often come down to this question: For what audience are we doing these things in these ways? This preaching, this visiting, this planning, this appearing at meetings. Whose approval do we seek? Whose criticism do we fear? For whom do we dress the way we do? For whom do we smile?

Clergymen are notorious for turning down many things because, as we say, "What would *my people* think?" It is astonishing how consistently "my people" means those most representative of what I have been calling the dominant culture. Jesus, who was also warned by others to watch out lest he offend his own people, reminded his critics that he had other sheep that were not of "this fold." Often he acted as radically as he did just for those outside the flock—the lost sheep, the alien, the rejected, the forsaken. Finally he could not do what he had come to do until he had become one of them himself, crucified outside the Holy City.

Strangely it was precisely because he achieved a reputation for befriending the "other sheep" that some of those in Israel's own fold also sought him out . . . secretly. Like Nicodemus.

Shepherds who become known for caution with respect to their own flock are often not available for the *real* problems even of their flock!

In the complex activities of daily life it is difficult to ascertain where we are dependent upon the dominant, "Middle" culture. Much of what we do is automatic, even mechanical. We naturally assume that board members should include the most influential persons in the church. If there is a choice between a professional man and a laborer, the laborer has to be exceptional in order to win. Recently the board of a congregation known to me was called to the front of the church to be presented to the congregation. It seemed as though every doctor, lawyer, and merchant chief in the congregation was on it! Both as ministers and as laymen we give symbols every day of our adherence to the dominant culture. And most of it is quite unknown to us.

In this respect, too, we are today in a more favorable position to become wise about our hidden assumptions. There are groups and individuals in our midst who feel a certain mission to teach us about these assumptions.

Why should we not invite them to do so? Why should we not sincerely ask for their help in detecting the ways in which we have identified the Christian life with certain social and cultural priorities?

Why should more churchmen not make it a point of Christian obedience to become involved in movements and organizations that are attempting to make meaningful protests against the Establishment? There could be no better way of learning to detect the Christian entanglement with the cultural ideology than by becoming familiar with what the protesting groups identify as Establishment. I suspect that the more we discovered about it, the more we would realize that we have indeed been part of it.

Seminarians, in their courses dealing with pastoral theology, have always been advised that they should

take an active part in the life of the community. Generation after generation of clergy have gone out into the
world convinced that this means becoming a member of
some civic committee, the horticultural society, a lodge
or service club, business or professional organization.
They sought identity with groups that represent the
majority interests of the community. Why have we assumed that involvement in the community always
means association with *those* organizations? It says a
great deal about our own priorities and our estimate of
the character of the church. There is today every reason
to think that the most significant public involvement
for clergy and active laymen would be in organizations
of a completely different sort, especially those which
are critical of the majority interests.

The disengagement from "Middle American" ideological assumptions, if it occurred on any significant
scale, could only be a very painful process in the
churches. It could not happen without suffering. If
taken seriously, no doubt it would mean a drastic drop
in church membership—at least a noticeable turnover.
That is frightening to many people. But our statistical
records have nothing to do with what really matters.
The power that we suppose we possess because of our
adherence to "doctors, lawyers, and merchant chiefs" is
a mirage of power. Why should we not risk an open and
clear-cut break! Not with people—though it may frequently seem to be that—but with what the people
represent, or think they represent.

Living Without the Constantinian Assumption

Not only are we called to disentangle the faith, and
ourselves as its representatives, from the ideological
moorings of the dominant classes; but beyond that we

are called to give up, altogether, the Constantinian assumption.

At this juncture in the history of the church it would
be a mistake to think that we would be doing the obedi-
ent thing if only we dissociated ourselves from the middle class. That is too simple. We must stop depending
on the dominant, "Middle" culture, with its particular
needs. We must also stop looking around for anybody
else to depend upon, any other group or social stratum.
We have to find an alternative to Christendom altogether.

One wonders: Is it simply nonsense to imagine that
the churches after all these centuries could actually *will*
the death of Christendom? That Christians could relinquish voluntarily *that* kind of working arrangement
with the world?

G. P. Baker in his book on Constantine relates that
when the emperor Galerius came to Nicomedia around
the year A.D. 302 to report that the foes of order and good
government had not yet been suppressed, he named
the Christian church as one such foe. Baker comments:

> In theory—or at any rate in principle—the Church had
> not even the right to exist. It was an illegal body,
> whose creed had only to be stated in order to demon-
> strate its unlawful nature. It acted as a corporation,
> though it was no corporation. It owned money and
> other chattels. . . . It was an alien and intrusive body,
> an *imperium in imperio*, counteracting the legal influence
> of properly constituted authorities, drawing away the
> obedience of citizens to a code of conduct and a scheme
> of ideas not endorsed by the government—imposing a
> law in supersession of the one constitutionally valid law
> of the sovran state. It was a seditious body. It was a
> conspiracy, a treason and a revolution.[80]

It is a long way from that to the "comfortable pew" of today's "Sunday, bloody Sunday"! Is it so far away that there could be no recovering of the revolutionary quality today? Must the revolution belong only to the few "token Christians"—the Berrigans, the Dom Helder Câmaras, the few who enter the ranks of marchers and protestors? Does the body of Christ in the more inclusive sense inevitably end up on the side of respectability, law and order, and the Disney World?

Perhaps it is too much to expect any significant search for an alternative style of worldly life on the part of the majority of those who presently constitute the churches. There are strong reasons, indeed, for despairing of the whole prospect. On the other hand, we should avoid being fatalized by past performance, and especially by anything that loads the dice from the outset with such a concept as "the majority." Let us be quite realistic: "The majority" are not going to make it into the future of the Christian church one way or another! Honesty demands that we drop that concept straightaway and ask, instead, about significant minorities: minorities that are significant because of something quite unrelated to their quantity.

It is possible, and highly so, that such a significant minority can be found today who are ready to will the death of Christendom. There are Christians who are anxious to direct this demise; to supervise it; to try to exercise some influence on what transpires during and after it, instead of merely allowing it to happen by default and then attempting to pick up the pieces.

A key factor in the thought of such a minority would have to be the economic one. If the form of Christendom has been permitted to linger long after the content of it has become ineffectual, it is certainly due in great measure to the favored economic status of the churches. This is more obvious in Western European establishments than in North America. But it is also true of us. In one smaller Canadian city, for example,

> with a population of 130,485, there are 92 Protestant and Orthodox and 13 Roman Catholic churches. The land and buildings owned by these churches is valued at almost $4 million. Based on the current mill rate, these churches get a property tax exemption of about $300,000.[81]

We may be of the opinion that such economic privileges as these go unnoticed. If so, we are thoroughly mistaken. There is, in fact, great resentment of these privileges even among citizens who are in other respects friendly enough toward institutional Christianity.

Many others, less charitable, find it hard to believe that the churches could be independent of the rest of the Establishment when they so clearly benefit in this way.

A church seeking to end the Constantinian arrangement voluntarily could do no better by way of a beginning than to relinquish, at its own suggestion, the economic privilege of tax exemption and other such privileges.

Certainly that could only be a beginning—in some ways a mere token of intent. Nevertheless, it is the sort of beginning that would necessitate *forthwith* further activities in the direction of disestablishment. For it would create a situation in which the whole question of the church's relation to society could no longer be avoided.

If such a procedure seems unthinkable—and no doubt it does to most churchmen—then consider the alternative: As membership in the institutional churches dwindles; as other religious and ethical-political organizations proliferate in our society and demand equal privileges; as the burden on taxpayers brought on by energy, food, and other crises increases; as welfare encompasses more and more of the work that was formerly the concern of the churches, will not these ecclesiastical privileges inevitably be called into question? Is it conceivable that such exemptions and rights will continue to be extended to the churches? Indefinitely?

The point is: When we do nothing about these things, when we will nothing but their quiet continuance, we are simply putting off until our children's generation decisions that we cannot bring ourselves to face.

As a Christian, I like to think that in the church at least it is possible for people to include in the circle of their responsibility also "the generations of those yet unborn." This largess of spirit seems patently impossible for the secular community, which regularly limits its thinking until the next election! But in the church our vision of Christ's community can and must be broader than that. It can and must encompass not only "the saints" who have gone before but also the coming ones.

Those "little flocks" of the future—the not-distant future—will face discouragement and temptations unknown to us. For their sake—rather, for the sake of the hope for which they may be able to stand in that world! —is it possible for us already to declare, in anticipated solidarity with them: "Here! We will share your lot willingly. In so doing, we hope to influence what you may inherit from us by way of a place in the world's memory and in its heart."

🐾 3 🐾

The Freedom of
the Disestablished Church

The "for" of "from + for"

Disestablishment also means freeing the church (for) something.

The pain of disengaging the remnants of Christendom *from* the culture may be great. But the freedom awaiting the church in the disestablished situation is worth a great deal of pain. There is no adequate way to describe the fullness of that freedom. I am choosing three aspects of it to comment on briefly. I am convinced that this freedom of the disestablished church for the service of God and man is inherent *within* our present situation. It is not merely a potential for some indeterminate future. It is available right now—*if* Christians are prepared to undertake it at this time. Hence the three aspects on which I want to reflect in order to illustrate this freedom arise out of the analysis undertaken in the first part of this study. In each instance, the potential "freedom for" entails a purging of the unreality of the churches by the reality of the gospel.

3 aspects of waiting freedom

Free for the Real Questions

#1 free to pursue questions

The church that had disentangled itself from the Constantinian mentality would be free to pursue the real questions present in our own time.

We have observed that many of the most basic questions of our epoch are being asked today *outside* the churches. Psychiatrists talk about sin. Novelists and young people are conscious of an apocalypse. Communist philosophers ask about the significance of Jesus for atheists. Sociologists see in modern technocracy the ghost of Mephistopheles. Biologists ask where we are going to draw the line in our supposed mastery of earth. The reason these questions are stated outside the churches, and find so little echo inside them, is that the churches are committed to a religion in which there must be no really dark themes.

To be more specific, only dark themes that are readily made light will be considered in the churches. We must be positive. We must be optimistic. We must maintain the illusion of human control—even if that means begging some pretty serious questions about the sovereignty of God. We deal in answers, not in questions. Look at the announcements on the church page in local newspapers: How to have a happy family life. How to overcome the problem of pollution. How to ensure good government. How to treat the aged. How to believe in God. How to have a meaningful life even though you are a single woman. How to get the most out of life. How to have . . . well, yes, eternal life!

Nicodemus has no questions that we are not prepared to answer.

Which means in translation: We are not prepared to meet any Nicodemuses who have questions that we are not prepared to answer!

A church that had been freed from the ideological assumptions on which this "positive religion" has been based would be a church deprived of this facility with answers. At least it would not have to keep up that reputation. For the Constantinian church to be without answers is an embarrassment. Power lies in the answer —or so it seems. In reality, when questions become too pressing, when men find themselves in the midst of complex dilemmas where there are no clear-cut alternatives, when "the experts" discover that for the deepest problems of society there are "no technical solutions"[82] —to say in such a time that one possesses answers is to invite laughter.

Ours is such a time. Instead of providing easy answers to everything, it would be better for the church to concentrate on being a place to which questions could be brought. There are very few such places in the contemporary world where the deepest and most disturbing questions can be put. To ask the question— merely to ask it—is for many people in our society the most difficult undertaking. Not only is it humiliating to ask, as it always has been, but with us today it is unnerving, because one suspects that no one *can* answer our most anxious questions. One fears that there are no answers, there are only questions. And if that is so, one thinks that it is better not to articulate such questions.

Still, the very articulation of the questions could be the beginning of a new courage. To live with unasked questions, to *be* the question one cannot ask, is a situation very close to ultimate despair. But if people are able to form their questions in the presence of one another, if a *community of questioners* becomes possible, would that not be close to the community of the cross?

Is it possible to be man in a world dominated by technique? Is meaning possible in a world that might end meaninglessly? "What are human beings *for?*"[83]

To be the place and the people where such rudimentary questions can be asked, lived out, reflected upon, shared, could in itself be the beginning of *real* community. Triumphalistic, answering theology finds such a proposal humiliating. But there is no entering into the koinonia of Jesus Christ which is not by way of humiliation, dying, being drowned in the baptismal waters. Genuine koinonia only begins for a man when he understands that he has nothing to bring to it except his emptiness and need. That includes also the realization that he is empty of wisdom, empty of answers. What prevents genuine koinonia from falling into sin, into the new hubris of ever-renewed quests for power and glory, is its being reduced ever and again to the status of the question mark. God robs us of our answers so that he may be among us as the Answer. Or perhaps as the Question: the Question that we can never answer and from whose grasp we can never fully escape.

To be the community of the question means not only to be "there" for the questions that men ask and are; it means also to be present in the world as witness to the question that *God* asks of all of man's activities.

Hans-Dieter Bastian, a German theologian who has worked out what he calls a theology of the question, reports that

> in August, 1968, after Russian troops had invaded Czechoslovakia, a Czech truck drove between the columns of soviet military vehicles. The truck carried a poster with the single Russian word "Why?" "It is the present task of Christianity," says Bastian, "to carry this poster polyglot through history. As long as war and terror, violence and indifference befall man daily, but God does not reach him, it will carry on and must continue to ask."[84]

To become a community where the question may be freely asked and where there is again courage to raise God's question mark over man and his kingdoms, this is to become a community that explores what Archbishop Temple called "a religion of redemption." Basically, all questions of ultimate concern are questions of redemption. "Can the world be saved?"

Christendom Christianity of the modern, North American variety has not been a religion of redemption. With the culture to which it was bound, it has assumed that redemption is a given of historical existence. Redemption is a matter of nature, not of grace. Salvation is built into the very structure of things. Everything is going to work itself out in our favor. God is on our side. What else could Christianity say, so long as its tune was being called by that particular patron?

To have disengaged ourselves from the officially optimistic society means to have recovered the possibility of entertaining a religion of redemption. In North American Protestantism it could mean discovering for the first time what the Protestant Reformers meant by "sheer grace" (*sola gratia*). Many of us could only be shocked by such a discovery. For the switch from nature to grace means finding out that nothing is guaranteed in advance. It is not a foregone conclusion that everything will work out in man's favor. Certainly not in terms of the way that modern man conceived the human future. And certainly not when the favorable future of mankind utterly ignored, as it did, the greater share of humanity—the "lesser breeds without the law." Nothing at all is promised with respect to the future in the religion of "sheer grace": only that God will be with us in life and in death.

If we understand that, we will be able again to raise the question of salvation, to stand for that question in the midst of our society, and to listen for it seriously when it is raised by those who do not frequent our sanctuaries. In other words, we will no longer be insulated from the question by the possession of an all-embracing answer.

Neither, in that case, will we be alienated from those in whom the question manifests itself so deeply in our world. It takes its most graphic, most appalling shape in the poor with their "Why?"; the oppressed with their "Why?"; the sick; the aged; the victims of war; the young—all of those whom we have been able heretofore to regard almost objectively, as objects of our charity, from the height of our "bourgeois transcendence" (Käsemann).

To be free for the question is to be free for those in whom the question appears.

Free to Be and to Befriend "The Alternative"

A church freed from service to a particular worldly authority is free for the service of all men, regardless of their ideologies, class, sex, or race. It is free to be vigilant for man, and to support those in whom ultimate concern for man's humanity is present.

One of the most disappointing aspects of the failure of the churches in our time has been their response to the two most significant movements of the past decade in North America: the Bohemian counter culture, and the activist protest of the '60s which called not only for an end to the war in Vietnam but also for a radical reform of institutions and entrenched attitudes.

These two movements were by no means identical,

nor were they necessarily compatible. As Philip Slater stated the difference: "One group seeks to redirect the old striving pattern to social goals—to build a revolutionary new society instead of empires and fortunes—while the other seeks to abolish the old striving pattern itself. One seeks to remake the world to make it tolerable for us to live in, the other tries to cure us of our need to remake the world."[85]

Both wings of the protesting movement, however, represented the attempt to explore an *alternative* to the route of technological man—the way of life that has become a way of death.

The whole counter-cultural movement, which was part of a revolution much deeper than these two groups, can be interpreted as Paul Tillich did in an essay written in 1959. The essay is called "Aspects of a Religious Analysis of Culture."[86]

"Our present culture," writes Tillich, "must be described in terms of one predominant movement and an increasingly powerful protest against this movement."[87] This predominant movement Tillich names "the spirit of industrial society." Today he would no doubt have used the more common terminology, "the technological society." He discusses the spirit of industrial society, as we have done earlier in this study, in the language of mastery. It is

the concentration of man's activities upon the methodological investigation and technical transformation of his world, including himself, and the consequent loss of the dimension of depth in his encounter with reality.[88]

Against this, the spirit of the protest is, for Tillich, the spirit of existentialist philosophy. "Existentialism,

Tillich, Theology of Culture

in the largest sense," Tillich claims, "is the protest against the spirit of industrial society, within the framework of industrial society."[89] The protest is made in behalf of man. It is

> directed against the position of man in the system of production and consumption of our society. Man is supposed to be the master of his world and of himself. But actually he has become a part of the reality he has created, an object among objects, a thing among things, a cog within a universal machine to which he must adapt himself in order not to be smashed by it. But this adaptation makes him a means for ends which are means themselves, and in which an ultimate end is lacking. Out of this predicament of man in the industrial society the experiences of emptiness and meaninglessness, of dehumanization and estrangement have resulted. Man has ceased to encounter reality as meaningful.[90]

The protesting element in society is "theologically significant," says Tillich, for it analyzes and portrays in our midst the predicament of man. It keeps before us the alternative to what has become dominant and what, if it is not curbed, will end by destroying the spirit of man.

In itself, the church does not have "the power to attack and to transform the spirit of industrial society." But insofar as it listens to those outside itself who are vigilant for man, it can help to shape the life of society.

> In its prophetic role the Church is the guardian who reveals dynamic structures in society and undercuts their demonic power by revealing them, even within the Church itself. In so doing the Church listens to prophetic voices outside itself, judging both the culture and the Church insofar as it is part of the culture. We have referred

to such prophetic voices in our culture. Most of them are not active members in the manifest Church. But perhaps one could call them participants of a "latent Church," a Church in which the ultimate concern which drives the manifest Church is hidden under cultural forms and deformations.[91]

It is the task of the church, says Tillich, to recognize in movements outside itself echoes of its own better traditions of concern for humanity. Often it has to be reminded of this concern for humanity by those who are beyond its own membership. It has then to reform itself according to what it hears from them, and to help give shape and direction to their prophetic concern:

> Sometimes this latent Church comes into the open. Then the manifest Church should recognize in these voices what its own spirit should be and accept them even if they appear hostile to the Church. But the Church should also stand as a guardian against the demonic distortions into which attacks must fall if they are not grasped by the right subject of our ultimate concern.[92]

This analysis of Tillich's is useful in assessing the role of the churches vis-à-vis the counter culture of the '60s. In that movement, we had a clear if amorphous instance of the spirit of protest against industrial society. Especially in its Bohemian wing, it would be quite accurate to link this movement with existentialism. It was "grassroots existentialism." Both wings of the movement, however, activist and Bohemian, represented an attempt to explore alternatives to the deadly course being followed by the dominant, technological culture.

The adherents of this protest were not always wise, for they were "improvising their own ideal of adulthood."[93] Their movement—if it can even be referred to in the singular—was like a great mass of energy, unformed, or only partially formed. It needed formation, direction.

In particular it needed to be put in touch with the best traditions of our own civilization. Even on their own, a surprising number of the young who were involved in the counter culture discovered something of the traditions of Jerusalem and Athens. I remember a young man who came to Canada in 1969—by label a draft dodger—who was very much a part of this movement. In the course of our initial conversations, I found out that he was well versed in the Scriptures (though he was not overtly religious), and that he was reading Plato as well. In Greek! I asked him: "How on earth did that happen? We did our best to keep these things from you!" He responded that we had made the mistake of leaving the Bible and some other books around on end tables and decorative bookshelves, he guessed for the impression they created of learning and morality.

For the most part, however, the counter culture received no help from those in the society best equipped to offer direction. It was certainly "without benefit of clergy." Neither the intellectual community, supposed heir of the tradition of Athens, nor the religious community, supposed heir of the tradition of Jerusalem, saw in this protesting movement any basic challenge to *its own* direction. Nor did either community see the movement as something to be supported, formed, refined, and cultivated as an alternative to the dehumanizing trends of the dominant culture. True, the religious community sometimes went so far as to put up hostels for these wandering "troubadours of the apocalypse" (Wiesel). That seemed in keeping with our official Christian brand of charity.

But as for the real charity, which blesses him who gives as well as him who takes, we were not capable of it. The churches were not free to identify with these counter-cultural thrusts, whether political or apolitical. On the contrary, they were bound to oppose them. For the churches had a previous commitment that made it necessary a priori to reject the counter culture.

That commitment was to the dominant culture against which the protesting movement was protesting. "We *are* the dominant culture!" cried a member of the board of a Christian seminary when he was presented with a document that proposed modeling theological education on the counter-cultural model. Of course he was perfectly right.

Being tied to the dominant, "Middle" culture—hardly distinguishable from that wallpaper—the churches are free neither to be nor to befriend authentic alternatives to that culture. They must reject every alternative, even when a particular alternative may indeed represent a prophetic function highly compatible with the true function of the church.

It is by now axiomatic that unless Western man is able to discover a life-style radically different from the one that modernity taught him to pursue, our civilization will end in catastrophe. It is no little thing, therefore, to ask whether the church is or is not free to be or to befriend real alternatives to that technocratic society. Our bondage to the dominant culture can be broken, at this juncture in history, only if enough Christians are able to achieve a vision of humanity broad enough to encompass not only the present but also the immediate future. To side with the dominant culture against the alternatives is to decide *against* the majority of the men of the future—against our own children. It would be ironic indeed if, in order to maintain our position of dubious favor with the majority culture today, we alienated ourselves entirely from the masses of tomorrow, whose lives will be severely circumscribed by the continuation of "our way of life."

A significant and articulate minority of "men of goodwill" today are seeking a way into the future. It is *possible* for Christians, out of the riches of the tradition of Jerusalem, to give a great deal of help along this way. There are few organizations in the contemporary world that can offer such help. The universities are even more tied to the apron strings of technocracy than are the churches. At the same time, the universities are not so beholden to their own traditional roots in the wisdom of Greece as are the churches to theirs in the wisdom of Jerusalem.

For all their waywardness, and in spite of their captivation by modernity, the churches still live with the tradition of Jerusalem; above all, they live with the Scriptures of the Jews and the early Christians. They have this link with the past, this entrée into a civilization that predates modernity. Even without guidance from the churches, many of the wisest and most sensitive persons of our epoch quite on their own have seen the pertinence of that tradition for their search for a way into the future. They recognize the significance of the tradition of Jerusalem, not only for its own intrinsic worth but also because it is in a special sense *our* (Western) past. They know that there is no getting beyond our present impasse which does not come to terms with that past and with the modern distortions of it.

Freed from a stratum of society that insists upon a certain well-known interpretation of the Christian tradition, the church would be free *for* the reinterpretation of that tradition in the light of the real problem of mankind today. It would not be bound to uphold a way of life that has become a way of death. It would be free to seek, in company with other men of goodwill, a real alternative: an alternative consistent with the Way of Him who came "that ye might have life."

Free to Hope

The church that had disengaged itself from the officially optimistic, dominant culture would be free to inquire anew into the possibility of hope in our time.

No one who really knows "what time it is" can doubt that the basic analysis of thinkers such as Moltmann, Alves, Metz, Wiesel, Fackenheim, and many others, is correct. Ours is a time when hope is most difficult, and most necessary.

Even Jacques Ellul, who has often been accused of sheer pessimism and courting the night, has written recently:

> The central question for man (and for the Christian) today is not whether to believe or not, but whether to hope or not. If someone says to me that a person obviously cannot hope in something he does not believe in, I reply that it is a matter of the dominant factor. In other words, for centuries hope has been defined in terms of faith (and rightly so). To believe in the Lord Jesus implied hoping for his return, the resurrection, etc. It is this relationship which now has to be turned around. . . .
>
> Today it is hope which is called upon to arouse, incite,

and induce faith; and to define it, that is to say, to give it content. Now, in the Christian life of today, we are called upon to believe what we hope. We must awaken people to hope, for only there can faith take root.[94]

I am prepared to think that the need for hope is today a *universal* need. It pertains as much to the affluent as to the destitute. For by now it is hardly possible for any thinking person to avoid the conclusion that in relation to the enormity of our problems and the scarcity of our resources we are all destitute. Affluence is just a little covering over our universal nakedness, a luxury in which a few are able to indulge for the time being. It may in fact be argued that hopelessness is *more* characteristic of the rich nations, for the very reason that they have been able to taste, for a few decades or centuries, something else.

Whoever knows man knows that it is not possible to live without hope. Perhaps an individual—perhaps a Camus—can determine to "think clearly and hope no more." But civilizations are *dependent* on expectancy. When that goes, the very heart of the culture has stopped beating. It is only a matter of time before death and putrification will become unbearable.

With the exception of the overt nihilists, we are all driven today by the necessity of discerning a basis for hope. Religious and nonreligious, ideologues and pragmatists, all are bound to ask and attempt to answer the question: Is hope possible or permitted in such a world as this?

Those of us who ask this question in North America are presented with a strange and difficult situation.

Here hope is a way of life. It is the very foundation stone of our New World. One has only to announce that he is seeking to promote *hope* and he will be welcomed with open arms. Well, of course! That is what we are all about! We are against pessimists; against artists with their distorted pictures, their *Guernica*s and the like; against that literature and drama which seems to have forgotten how to portray life whole and wholesome; against gloomy scientists who speak of the death of oceans and ecosystems; against intellectuals who pick us apart and call us "repressive"; against the young who reject the good life their parents have worked so hard to obtain for them. We stand against all these destructive elements. Let us by all means have more people who build up the positive foundations and values of our society. Let us by all means emphasize the necessity of being hopeful.

Thus the very optimism of our official culture is the greatest barrier to the recovery of authentic hope.

Really to hope in our time means to hope as do those who stand at the edge of the Red Sea. But the official optimism of the dominant culture precludes any such vision of our situation. We are not permitted to think so *negatively* as to believe that we have come to an impasse!

Our problem is: How can we instill hope in a people who do not permit themselves to acknowledge their own despair?

That these people are in a state of despair can no longer be reasonably doubted. We have demonstrated our despair openly—for all the world to see. Every news broadcast contains the implicit cry, "See—how we despair of life!"

But our greatest despair is that we cannot admit our despair.

So desperate are we to suppress our desperation that we will turn every occasion into an excuse for celebrating the positive grounds of our culture. The churches are at the heart of this desperate attempt to celebrate. Their unreality, as we have seen earlier, stems precisely from their function as sanctuaries against the night.

Perhaps they will be successful, in their own ways of measuring success, so long as they are able to serve the sanctuary function well for a significant segment of the population. So long as they can seem to stand for what is lovely and of good report; so long as they can make men believe, if only for an hour or so on Sundays, that faith, hope, and charity are possible in this world without changing anything very drastically; so long as they can add their religious sanction to the fond dreams of progress and technological salvation, they will not become quite empty.

But precisely so long as they pursue *that* course they will keep authentic hope at bay. Instead of real hope, they will be pursuing the same fantastic optimism that has brought us as a people to this present state of immaturity and hidden despair. For there are none so immature as those who close their eyes to all the data of despair in order to be able to hope.

There is no hope for us that does not lie through the valley of the shadow of death. We citizens of the United States and Canada shall learn to hope only insofar as we submit ourselves openly to the hidden despair that in-

forms our entire civilization. We have learned how to
boast about our past. We shall now have to learn to read
it more carefully. It is a past full of pretensions and
shallowness. If there was greatness in it, it was also full
of the seeds of failure from the beginning. Like Israel
at the edge of the Red Sea, we shall have to discover that
there is neither a way ahead nor a way back. Only then
will hope become a real possibility for us.

The church that has been able to disentangle itself
from its cultural captivity could begin to explore the
possibility of such hope. *Only* by disestablishing itself
could the church avail itself of such an opportunity.
Commitment to the dominant culture means, willy-
nilly, commitment to the optimism that can never learn
hope in the Christian sense of the word, the hope that
is against hope (Rom., ch. 4).

One test of genuine disestablishment in such a society as ours must be whether our Christianity serves
to *introduce us* to the data of despair. Is it possible in the
context of the congregation to hear and to reflect upon
the fact that as a people we have failed? That we are part
of the problem, not its answer? That we are the thieves,
not the good Samaritans? Is it possible to go away from
the service of worship without "feeling good," without
answers, perhaps even burning with some terrible questions that had not occurred to us before? Having given
our mite or our tithe, have we still the distinct impression that there is very little that we can "do"? Do we fly
to this sanctuary for refuge? Or does it begin to seem
that the world itself offers better sanctuaries than the
church?

To be laid open to the despair that is in fact silently

eating away at us is not the end of the matter. But it is the only means to authentic hope—at least where North Americans and North American Christians are concerned. Until we have entertained the problem in all of its complexity, including our own complicity in it, we shall not be able to entertain the hope that mankind may yet be permitted to pass through the midst of the sea. The only hope that is worth having is the hope that comes to those who sit in darkness and in the shadow of death.

Conclusion

Disestablishment along such lines as these is possible. It is not *necessary*. On the basis of past performance, one is tempted to predict that there will be no transformation of Christianity from "Christendom" to "the diaspora," but a complete absence of decisive action. The Christendom situation will be allowed to continue, however superficially, until it has become altogether untenable and ridiculous. By that time only a few will care, in any case, what happens to the churches. In many places today—in old downtown churches, in village and small-town parishes, and elsewhere—this impression is already clearly communicated by the immobility and lethargy of the remnant that remains.

Only one thing can make the difference between the slow death of Christendom and the possibility of a deliberate, purposeful choice of "the diaspora." That is a renewed vision, shared by a significant minority of people in the churches, of the reality of the gospel which has been entrusted to the church.

We are quite beyond the point where people could be roused to save the churches for their own sakes. This fact is well attested by the decline of interest in the ecumenical movement, which became too much identified with ecclesiastical and denominational self-preservation. But if it begins to seem necessary that the gospel be heard again in the world, then it is possible that the church can be re-formed around that reality.

I have argued that there is indeed reason to believe that many people today think the gospel is capable of addressing the real world. If there is a future for the churches, it will only be if and insofar as they are able to permit themselves to be conformed to that gospel.

Why should that surprise us or alarm us? If we are amazed at such a prospect, surely it is only because we have forgotten that the church always was formed around the gospel, not vice versa. Perhaps sixteen centuries of the Christendom mentality has really succeeded in creating the impression that the church precedes and possesses the gospel. In that case, the end of Christendom could be for us the beginning of a whole new adventure with the Spirit of God in the world.

At the end of his provocative study of the nineteenth century, Karl Löwith comments as follows on the thought of J. C. Overbeck:

> Whoever will take the trouble to pursue Overbeck's train of thought will perceive in the labyrinth of his sentences, so full of reservations, the straight and daring line of an absolutely honest mind. He elucidated the problem which Christianity presents for us. In the typical figures of the nineteenth century, he made clear the abyss separating us from Christianity. Since Hegel, and particularly through the work of Marx and Kierkegaard, the Christianity of this

bourgeois-Christian world has come to an end. This does not mean that a faith which once conquered the world perishes with its last secular manifestations. For how should the Christian pilgrimage *in hoc saeculo* ever become homeless in the land where it has never been at home.[95]

I can think of no period in history when it could have been more significant to be a member of the Christian koinonia. It is possible at this juncture in time, after centuries of self-deception, really to believe in the New Testament's own picture of the church: a pinch of salt, a bit of yeast, a little light in a black and extensive night, a small city on a hilltop. Nothing grand. But something real, all the same.

We have also this advantage: that we have already tried the way of grandeur. In the wake of its failure, we may at last be ready to resist the third temptation of Christ. After sixteen centuries of courting "the kingdoms of this world and the glory of them," we may be prepared to recognize that the way of grandeur is not the way of the Christ.

Besides, at crucial points of its self-awareness, the world itself has begun to question the pursuit of glory. At the pinnacle of its Babel quest for permanence and significance, the world today has found cause to wonder whether a humbler vision might not have been more fitting. Modern technology has provided us with ships that reach up into the heavens and down into the depths of the universe, and with machines that almost think. Nothing has ever been so triumphant as the technological achievements of contemporary man. Yet none of it can save us. Perhaps it is killing us.

Today, therefore, anxious men yearn for a little light, a little wisdom, a little love. In the night they ask about the meaning of life. "What are human beings *for?*"

Around that yearning and that asking, Jesus Christ will yet build his church.

Notes

CHAPTER 1

THE REALITY OF THE GOSPEL

1. Gerald J. Jud, Edgar W. Mills, and Genevieve Walters Burch (eds.), *Ex-Pastors: Why Men Leave the Parish Ministry* (Pilgrim Press, 1970), p. 5.

2. Paul Ehrlich and Anne Ehrlich, *Population, Resources, Environment: Issues in Human Ecology* (W. H. Freeman & Company, Publishers, 1970), p. 324.

3. Quoted in Alec Vidler, *20th Century Defenders of the Faith* (London: SCM Press, Ltd., 1965), pp. 81–82.

4. Gabriel Marcel, *Man Against Mass Society*, tr. by G. S. Fraser (Henry Regnery Company, Gatewood Editions, 1971), p. 13.

5. Cf. B. F. Skinner, *Beyond Freedom and Dignity* (Alfred A. Knopf, Inc., 1971).

6. Cf. Norman Mailer, *Fire on the Moon* (New American Library, Signet Books, 1971).

7. Josef Čapek and Karel Čapek, *R.U.R. and The Insect Play*, tr. by P. Selver (Oxford University Press, 1961). Reprinted by

permission of Oxford University Press.

8. The last written words of Martin Luther.

9. "Art in all its forms can show three states of mind: hopelessness, foolish hope, and genuine hope. If we look at our present artistic creations we find that artistic expressions of hopelessness by far prevail. . . . Artistic interpretations of genuine hope . . . are rare today." (Paul Tillich, "The Right to Hope," *University of Chicago Magazine,* Nov. 1965, p. 19.)

10. Hermann Hesse, *Steppenwolf,* tr. by Basil Creighton, rev. by Joseph Mileck and Horst Frenz (Holt, Rinehart & Winston, Inc., 1968), p. 21.

11. A. J. Heschel, *Who Is Man?* (Stanford University Press, 1966), p. 24.

12. M. Block and Robert G. Shedd (eds.), *Masters of Modern Drama* (Random House, Inc., 1965), p. 1113.

13. Theodore Roszak, *The Making of a Counter-Culture: Reflections on the Technological Society and Its Youthful Opposition* (Doubleday & Company, Inc., Anchor Books, 1969).

14. Karl Menninger, M.D., *Whatever Became of Sin?* (Hawthorn Books, Inc., 1973), p. 1. Quotations from this work are reprinted by permission of Hawthorn Books, Inc.

15. *Ibid.,* p. 5.

16. *Ibid.,* p. 227.

17. *Ibid.,* pp. 227–228. (Italics added.)

18. George P. Grant, *Technology and Empire: Perspectives on North America* (Toronto: House of Anansi, 1969), p. 118.

19. Skinner, *Beyond Freedom and Dignity.*

20. Quoted in Basil Willey, *The Seventeenth Century Background* (Doubleday & Company, Inc., Anchor Books, 1953), pp. 95–96.

21. Cf., e.g., Heidegger's "Memorial Address" on the occasion of the 175th birthday of the composer Konradin Kreutzer, in *Discourse on Thinking,* tr. by John M. Anderson and E. Hans Freund (Harper & Row, Publishers, Inc., 1966).

22. Cf., e.g., Josef Pieper, *Hope and History* (Herder & Herder, Inc., 1969).

23. Philip Slater, *The Pursuit of Loneliness: American Culture at the Breaking Point* (Beacon Press, Inc., 1970).

24. Jacques Ellul, *The Technological Society*, tr. by John Wilkinson (Alfred A. Knopf, Inc., 1964).

25. Rubem Alves, *Tomorrow's Child* (Harper & Row, Publishers, Inc., 1972), p. 14.

26. Cf., e.g., Marshall I. Goldman, *The Spoils of Progress: Environmental Pollution in the Soviet Union* (M. I. T. Press, 1972).

27. Alves, *Tomorrow's Child*, p. 20.

28. Kurt Vonnegut, *The Sirens of Titan* (Dell Publishing Co., 1970), pp. 274–275.

29. Ellul, *The Technological Society*, p. 16.

30. Cf. George Grant, *Time as History* (Toronto: Canadian Broadcasting Corporation, 1969), p. 34.

31. Mailer, *Fire on the Moon*, p. 48.

32. René Dubos, "Miracle of Health," in John G. Burke (ed.), *The New Technology and Human Values* (Wadsworth Publishing Company, Inc., 1966), p. 309.

33. Robert W. Funk (ed.), *Apocalypticism* (Herder & Herder, Inc., 1969), pp. 17 ff.

34. Karl Jaspers, *The Future of Mankind* (The University of Chicago Press, 1961), p. 5.

35. Roszak, *The Making of a Counter-Culture*, p. 43.

36. Rachel L. Carson, *Silent Spring* (Fawcett World Library, 1967), p. 12.

37. Frank Fraser Darling, reprinted in *The Listener*, Nov. 27, 1969.

38. James D. Ray, Jr., and Gideon E. Nelson (eds.), *What a Piece of Work Is Man: Introductory Readings in Biology* (Little, Brown & Company, 1971), p. 173.

39. *Ibid.*, p. 181.

40. Burke (ed.), *The New Technology and Human Values*, p. 8.

41. Donella H. Meadows *et al.*, *The Limits to Growth* (Universe Books, Inc., 1972).

42. Klaus Müller, *Die präparierte Zeit: Der Mensch in der Krise*

seiner eigenen Zielsetzungen (Stuttgart: Radius-Verlag, 1972).

43. Barbara Ward and René Dubos, *Only One Earth: The Care and Maintenance of a Small Planet* (London: André Deutsch, 1972), p. 298.

44. *Ibid.*

45. Maurice Zeitlin (ed.), *Father Camilo Torres: Revolutionary Writings* (Harper & Row, Publishers, Inc., Colophon Books, 1972), p. 317.

46. Sonia Orwell and Ian Angus (eds.), *Collected Essays, Journalism and Letters of George Orwell* (Penguin Books, 1970), Vol. 2, p. 30.

47. John C. Bennett, in *Christianity and Crisis*, Vol. XXIX, No. 16 (Sept. 29, 1969), p. 241.

48. Grant, *Time as History*, p. 31.

CHAPTER 2

The Unreality of the Churches

49. Jud, Mills, and Burch (eds.), *Ex-Pastors: Why Men Leave the Parish Ministry.*

50. Jacques Ellul, *Hope in Time of Abandonment*, tr. by C. Edward Hopkin (The Seabury Press, Inc., 1973), p. 73.

51. Karl Barth, *How to Serve God in a Marxist Land* (Association Press, 1959), p. 64.

52. "For almost a thousand years the chief force in western civilization was Christianity. Then, in about the year 1725, it suddenly declined and in intellectual society practically disappeared. Of course it left a vacuum. People couldn't get on without a belief in something outside themselves, and during the next hundred years they concocted a new belief, which, however irrational it may seem to us, has added a good deal to our civilization: a belief in the divinity of nature." (Kenneth Clark, *Civilisation* [London: British Broadcasting Corporation and John Murray, 1969], p. 269.)

53. Søren Kierkegaard, *Attack Upon Christendom*, tr. by Walter Lowrie (Beacon Press, Inc., 1944), p. 277.

54. Ellul, *Hope in Time of Abandonment*, p. 132.

55. Yves Congar, *Power and Poverty in the Church*, tr. by Jennifer Nicholson (Helicon Press, Inc., 1964), p. 127.

56. Jud, Mills, and Burch (eds.), *Ex-Pastors: Why Men Leave the Ministry*, p. 29.

57. Karl Rahner, *Mission and Grace*, tr. by Cecily Hastings (London: Sheed & Ward, Ltd., 1963), p. 20.

58. *Ibid.*, p. 25.

59. *Ibid.*

60. *Ibid.*, p. 34.

61. It is, however, in my view, giving way noticeably in these days to a far less confident image—perhaps one of bewilderment.

62. Our fascination for the nineteenth century is partly due to the fact that during it we reached a certain apex as a society; but partly also, as Paul Tillich frequently observed, because North America "never had a nineteenth century." By that he meant, I think, that we never experienced the chief *cultural* thrust of the nineteenth century, i.e., the romantic movement. There is a strange tension between these two things; for at the heart of the romantic movement was a protest against the very spirit of the nineteenth century which moved our society most, i.e., the spirit of industrialism. There is therefore a certain justification for our present, somehow nostalgic attachment to the nineteenth century, as evidenced, for instance, in the Bohemian wing of the counter culture. But I have the impression that when the churches hearken again to "nineteenth-century sentiments" they do so, not in the attempt to align themselves with the Romantic protest against industrialism, but in order to regain some vestige of the enthusiasm evidenced in Christianity on this continent during that period.

63. Albert H. van den Heuvel, *The Humiliation of the Church* (The Westminster Press, 1966), p. 51.

64. Jaspers, *The Future of Mankind*, p. viii.

65. Kurt Vonnegut, *God Bless You, Mr. Rosewater: Or Pearls Before Swine* (Dell Publishing Co., Delta Books, 1965), pp. 29–30.

66. Michael Novak, *The Experience of Nothingness* (Harper & Row, Publishers, Inc., Colophon Books, 1970), pp. 50 f.

67. Sidney Pollard, *The Idea of Progress* (London: Routledge & Kegan Paul, Ltd., 1958), p. 203.

68. Grant, *Technology and Empire*, p. 17.

69. Martin Buber wrote: "These last years in a great searching and questioning, seized ever anew by the shudder of the now, I have arrived no further than that I now distinguish a revelation through the hiding of the face, a speaking through the silence. The eclipse of God can be seen with one's eyes, it will be seen. He, however, who today knows nothing other than to say, 'See there, it grows lighter!' he leads to error." (Quoted in Emil Fackenheim, *God's Presence in History* [New York University Press, 1970], p. 61.)

70. Robert Heilbronner, *The Future as History* (Charles Scribner's Sons, 1959), p. 34.

71. Reinhold Niebuhr, *Faith and History* (Charles Scribner's Sons, 1951), p. 31.

72. An advertisement of Eastern Airlines.

CHAPTER 3

THE SPIRIT TO THE CHURCHES:
DISESTABLISH YOURSELVES!

73. Paul Kilborne, "Where the Church Is Real: Encounters with Christians and Others in East Germany." Unpublished manuscript. Used by permission.

74. Charles Davis, *A Question of Conscience* (London: Hodder & Stoughton, Ltd., 1967).

75. Karl Barth, *Dogmatics in Outline*, tr. by G. T. Thomson

(London: SCM Press, Ltd., 1949), p. 145.

76. The fact is that many of those who seek out Christian pastors, chaplains, and professors behind the Iron Curtain *are* Marxists. And very often they come, quite literally, at night. There is a growing interest in Christian teaching on the part of many Communists. One of the most widely read books of theology in West Germany during the past two years has been that of the Prague Marxist philosopher Milan Machovec, *Jesus für Atheisten* (Jesus for Atheists) (Stuttgart: Kreuz-Verlag, 1972).

77. Johannes Hamel, *A Christian in East Germany*, tr. by Ruth and Charles West (London: SCM Press, Ltd., 1960), p. 28.

78. As is well known, the first Christians were not called Christians but followers of "The Way." They were *in Via*, a *Communio Viatorum*.

79. Rahner, *Mission and Grace*, pp. 50–51.

80. G. P. Baker, *Constantine the Great: And the Christian Revolution* (Barnes & Noble, Inc., 1931), pp. 72–73.

81. B. G. Smillie, "He Says the Church Is Cheating," *The United Church Observer*, March 1971, p. 13.

82. The reference is to a key phrase in the well-known essay of the biologist Garrett Hardin, "The Tragedy of the Commons," reprinted in various sources, e.g., Robert Leo Smith, *The Ecology of Man: An Ecosystem Approach* (Harper & Row, Publishers, Inc., 1972), pp. 382 ff.

83. Cf. fn. 17, Ch. III, in Vonnegut, *God Bless You, Mr. Rosewater*.

84. Terrance Shillington, "Mission in Today's World." Unpublished S.T.M. thesis. (The reference is to Bastian's *Theologie der Frage* [Munich, 1969].)

85. Slater, *The Pursuit of Loneliness*, p. 124.

86. Paul Tillich, *Theology of Culture* (Oxford University Press, 1959), pp. 40 ff.

87. *Ibid.*, p. 43.

88. *Ibid.*

89. *Ibid.*, p. 46.

90. *Ibid.*

91. *Ibid.*, pp. 50–51.

92. *Ibid.*, p. 51.

93. Roszak, *The Making of a Counter-Culture*, p. 33.

94. Ellul, *Hope in Time of Abandonment*, pp. 88–89.

95. Karl Löwith, *From Hegel to Nietzsche: The Revolution in Nineteenth-Century Thought*, tr. by David E. Green (Holt, Rinehart & Winston, Inc., 1964), p. 388.